California Legal Research

Carolina Academic Press
Legal Research Series

Suzanne E. Rowe, Series Editor
ﾞﾟ

Arizona — Tamara S. Herrera

Arkansas — Coleen M. Barger

California — Hether C. Macfarlane & Suzanne E. Rowe

Colorado — Robert Michael Linz

Connecticut — Jessica G. Hynes

Florida, Third Edition — Barbara J. Busharis & Suzanne E. Rowe

Georgia — Nancy P. Johnson, Elizabeth G. Adelman & Nancy J. Adams

Idaho — Tenielle Fordyce-Ruff & Suzanne E. Rowe

Illinois, Second Edition — Mark E. Wojcik

Iowa — John D. Edwards, M. Sara Lowe, Karen L. Wallace
& Melissa H. Weresh

Kansas — Joseph A. Custer & Christopher L. Steadham

Louisiana — Mary Garvey Algero

Massachusetts — E. Joan Blum

Michigan, Second Edition — Pamela Lysaght & Cristina D. Lockwood

Minnesota — Suzanne Thorpe

Missouri, Second Edition — Wanda M. Temm & Julie M. Cheslik

New York — Elizabeth G. Adelman & Suzanne E. Rowe

North Carolina — Scott Childs

Ohio — Katherine L. Hall & Sara Sampson

Oregon, Second Edition — Suzanne E. Rowe

Pennsylvania — Barbara J. Busharis & Bonny L. Tavares

Tennessee — Sibyl Marshall & Carol McCrehan Parker

Texas — Spencer L. Simons

Washington, Second Edition — Julie Heintz-Cho, Tom Cobb
& Mary A. Hotchkiss

Wisconsin — Patricia Cervenka & Leslie Behroozi
ﾞﾟ

California Legal Research

Hether C. Macfarlane

Suzanne E. Rowe

Suzanne E. Rowe, Series Editor

Carolina Academic Press

Durham, North Carolina

Library of Congress Cataloging-in-Publication Data

Macfarlane, Hether C.
 California legal research / Hether C. Macfarlane, Suzanne E.
Rowe.
   p. cm.
 Includes bibliographical references and index.
 ISBN 978-1-59460-403-4 (alk. paper)
 1. Legal research--California. I. Rowe, Suzanne E., 1961- II.
Title.
 KFC74.M33 2008
 340.072'0794--dc22

                                          2008029217

Carolina Academic Press
700 Kent Street
Durham, North Carolina 27701
Telephone (919) 489-7486
Fax (919) 493-5668
www.cap-press.com

Printed in the United States of America.

Dedicated

to Stephen and Ellen
H.C.M.

and to Didi Alfred
S.E.R.

Summary of Contents

Contents

List of Tables and Figures

Series Note

The Legal Research Series published by Carolina Academic Press includes an increasing number of titles from states around the country. The goal of each book is to provide law students, practitioners, paralegals, college students, laypeople, and librarians with the essential elements of legal research in each state. Unlike more bibliographic texts, the Legal Research Series books seek to explain concisely both the sources of state law research and the process for conducting legal research effectively.

Preface and Acknowledgments

This book fills a niche in the literature available for California state law research by explaining not just the sources of law but the process of conducting research using those sources. The book should be valuable to a wide range of audiences—from first-year students to seasoned veterans.

Writing the book was a collaborative effort, with each author contributing to each chapter. The chapters on cases and secondary sources we wrote in tandem. Hether Macfarlane took primary responsibility for chapters on constitutions, statutes, administrative law, and legislative history. Suzanne Rowe drafted chapters on research techniques, updating, research strategies, and citation. Portions of this book reflect her work on other titles in the Legal Research Series.

We have been fortunate to have the support of many people as we wrote this book. For substantive review of the text, we are grateful to Dragomir Cosanici (California citation), Dan Galpern (legislative history), and Harvey Rogers. For research, editing, and administrative assistance, we appreciate the work of Kelly Fahl, Jeff Hinman, Chad Marriott, Jason Poss, Greena Ng, Harvey Rogers, Ben Albers, and Donna Williamson.

We recognize West and LexisNexis for permission to reproduce portions of their books and online products. Please note that further reproduction is prohibited.

Hether C. Macfarlane
Suzanne E. Rowe

California Legal Research

Chapter 1

The Research Process and Legal Analysis

I. California Legal Research

The fundamentals of legal research are the same in every American jurisdiction, though the details vary. While some variations are minor, others require specialized knowledge of the resources available and the analytical framework in which those resources are used. This book focuses on the resources and analysis required to be thorough and effective in researching California law. It supplements this focus with brief explanations of federal research and research into the law of other states, both to introduce other resources and to highlight some of the variations.

II. The Intersection of Legal Research and Legal Analysis

The basic process of legal research is often quite simple. For most print resources, you will begin with an index, find entries that appear relevant, read those sections of the text, and then find out whether more recent information is available. For most online research, you will search particular websites or databases using words likely to appear in the text of relevant documents.

Legal analysis is interwoven throughout this process, raising challenging questions. In print research, which words will you look up in the index? How will you decide whether an index entry looks promising? With online research, how will you choose relevant words and construct a search most likely to produce the documents you need? When you read the text of a document, how will you determine whether it is relevant to your client's situation? How will you learn whether more recent material changed the law or merely applied it in a new situation? The answer to each of these questions requires legal analysis. This intersection of research and analysis can make legal research very difficult, especially for the novice. While this book's focus is legal research, it also includes the fundamental aspects of legal analysis required to conduct research competently.

This book is not designed to be a blueprint of every resource in the law library or search engine on the Internet; many resources contain their own detailed explanations in a preface or a "Help" section. This book is more like a manual or field guide, introducing the resources needed at each step of the research process and explaining how to use them. Most readers will use the book most effectively by taking it to the library, where they can view the resources being explained, or by visiting the referenced sites on a computer.

III. Types of Legal Authority

The goal of legal research is to find constitutional provisions, statutes, administrative rules, and judicial opinions that control a client's situation. In other words, you are searching for primary, mandatory authority.

Law is often divided along two lines. The first line distinguishes primary authority from secondary authority. *Primary authority* is law produced by government bodies with law-making power. Legislatures write statutes, courts write judicial opinions, and administrative agencies write regulations. *Secondary authority* includes all other legal sources, such as treatises, law review articles, and legal encyclopedias. They may be written by attorneys and judges, by the editorial staff of publishing companies, or by law students. These secondary sources are designed to aid the researcher in understanding the law and locating primary authority.

Table 1-1. Examples of Authority in California Research

	Mandatory Authority	Persuasive Authority
Primary Authority	California statutes California Supreme Court cases California regulations	Washington statutes Oregon Supreme Court cases Nevada regulations
Secondary Authority	—	Law review articles Legal encyclopedias Treatises Restatements

Another division is made between mandatory and persuasive authority. *Mandatory authority* is binding on the court that would decide a conflict if the situation were litigated. In a question of California law, mandatory or binding authority includes California's constitution, statutes enacted by the California Legislature, opinions of the Supreme Court of California,[1] and California administrative rules. *Persuasive authority* is not binding, but may be followed if relevant and well reasoned. Authority may be merely persuasive if it is from a different jurisdiction or if it is not produced by a law-making body. In a question of California law, examples of persuasive authority would include a similar Washington statute, an opinion of an Oregon state court, and a law review article. Notice in Table 1-1 that persuasive authority may be either primary or secondary authority, while mandatory authority is always primary.

Within primary, mandatory authority, there is an interlocking hierarchy of law involving constitutions, statutes, administrative rules, and judicial opinions. The constitution of each state is the supreme law of that state. If a statute is on point, that statute comes next in the hierarchy, followed by administrative rules. Judicial

1. An opinion from the Court of Appeals is binding on the trial courts if the Supreme Court of California has not addressed a particular topic. *See Auto Equity Sales, Inc. v. Super. Ct. of Santa Clara Co.*, 57 Cal. 2d 450, 455–456 (1962). If the districts conflict, the trial court in a district without precedent is free to choose among the conflicting decisions.

opinions may interpret the statute or rule, but they cannot disregard either. A judicial opinion may, however, decide that a statute violates the constitution or that a rule oversteps its bounds. If there is no constitutional provision, statute, or administrative rule on point, the issue will be controlled by *common law*, also called judge-made law.[2]

IV. Overview of the Research Process

Conducting effective legal research means following a process. This process leads to the authority that controls a legal issue as well as to commentary that may help you analyze new and complex legal matters. The outline in Table 1-2 presents the basic research process.

A. Generating Research Terms

Legal research often begins with a list of words that are relevant to the topic of the research project. This list is important in both print and online resources. Many legal resources in print use lengthy indexes as the starting point for finding legal authority. Electronic sources often require the researcher to enter words that are likely to appear in a synopsis, a table of contents, or the full text of relevant documents. To ensure you are thorough in beginning a research project, you will need a comprehensive list of words, terms, and phrases that may lead to law on point. These may be legal terms or common words that describe the client's situation. The items on this list are *research terms*.

Organized brainstorming is the best way to compile a comprehensive list of research terms. Some researchers ask the journalistic questions: Who? What? How? Why? When? Where? Others use a mnemonic device like TARPP, which stands for Things, Actions,

---

2. Common law is derived from judicial decisions, rather than statutes or constitutions. *Black's Law Dictionary* 293 (Bryan A. Garner ed., 8th ed., West 2004).

Table 1-2. Overview of the Research Process

1. Generate a list of *research terms*.
2. Consult *secondary sources* and practice aids, including treatises, legal encyclopedias, and law review articles.
3. Find any controlling *constitutional provisions* and *statutes*.
4. Find any controlling *administrative regulations* and related administrative law.
5. Gather citations to relevant *cases* by reviewing secondary sources, annotated statutes, and digests (print indexes for cases), and by searching online topical databases. Read the cases either online or in print reporters.
6. Use *citators* to update or "Shepardize" your legal authorities to ensure they have not been repealed, reversed, modified, or otherwise changed.
7. In general, your *research is complete* when there are no holes remaining in your outline and when searches in different sources produce the same set of authorities.

Remedies, People, and Places. Whether you use one of these suggestions or develop your own method, generate a broad range of research terms regarding the facts, issues, and desired solutions of your client's situation. Include in the list both specific and general words. Try to think of synonyms and antonyms for each term since at this point you are uncertain which terms an index may include. Using a legal dictionary or thesaurus may help to generate additional terms.

As an example, assume a client has suffered nightmares and anxiety attacks after the following scene at a restaurant. He and his wife were having lunch at an outside table near the street. The man went inside to use the restroom, and as he returned to the table he heard a car crash. He saw a table umbrella fall and felt pieces of glass from a falling mirror. A car had jumped the curb and hit his wife. Although she eventually recovered from her serious injuries, he has continued to suffer symptoms. You wonder whether he has a claim for negligent infliction of emotion distress against the driver, although he was merely an ob-

Table 1-3. Generating Research Terms
Journalistic Approach

Who:	Driver, spouse, husband, bystander
What:	Car accident, lingering symptoms, anxiety, nightmares
How:	Being near accident that injured spouse
Why:	Reckless driving, witnessing accident
When:	Daytime, lunch hour
Where:	Restaurant, San Diego, street side, near sidewalk

server or bystander to the accident. Table 1-3 provides examples of research terms you might use to begin work on this project.

As your research progresses, you will learn new research terms to include in the list and decide to take others off. For example, in reading a secondary source you may learn a *term of art*, a word or phrase that has special meaning in a particular area of law. Or you may read cases that give you insights into the key words judges tend to use in discussing this topic. These words need to be added to the list.

B. Searching Secondary Sources

Most lawyers begin researching an unfamiliar area of law by turning to secondary sources. These sources include law review articles, encyclopedia entries, and books written by practicing attorneys. Secondary sources are helpful because they summarize, explain, and sometimes analyze the law. Often a secondary source will be easier to understand than a statute or a judicial opinion. Secondary sources are also helpful because they contain references to relevant statutes, regulations, cases, and other legal material.

C. Finding Constitutional Provisions and Statutes

California's constitution is the highest legal authority on state matters. It begins with fundamental rights that are similar to those ensured by the federal constitution. Article I of the California Constitution provides, "All people are by nature free and independent and have inalienable rights. Among these are enjoying and defending life and liberty, acquiring, possessing, and protecting property, and pursuing and obtaining safety, happiness, and privacy." But the constitution is not identical to the federal constitution, and it contains provisions that are more statutory in nature. For example, Article 10B of the constitution is known as the Marine Resources Protection Act of 1990; it prohibits the use of gill nets and trammel nets in certain zones.

The California Legislature has enacted statutes on many topics. Statutes are organized by subject matter in 29 codes ranging from "Civil Procedure" to "Labor" to "Revenue and Taxation." A list of the 29 codes is provided in Chapter 5 at Table 5-2. An example of a single statute is section 451 of the Penal Code, which sets the penalties for arson (Figure 5-4).

D. Researching Administrative Law

California has over 200 state regulatory agencies. These agencies issue regulations on matters ranging from drivers' licenses to environmental protection. The regulations are codified in 29 titles in the California Code of Regulations.[3] Agencies also decide disputes regarding the agencies' regulations. Although few law school courses address administrative law, it is a significant area of law and must be considered in a complete research process.

E. Researching Judicial Opinions

Courts write judicial opinions to explain their decisions in the cases that come before them. Some opinions are based on statutory law; the courts in these cases apply the statutory requirements to the facts of the parties before them. Other opinions are based on administrative law; most often, these cases are appeals from decisions

---

3. There is no one-to-one correspondence between the statutory code and the administrative code even though both have 29 chapters.

by administrative agencies. When no statute or administrative rule controls, judicial opinions are based on the common law.

Judicial opinions are published in rough chronological order in books called *reporters*. There are multiple reporters for California opinions, which will be covered in Chapter 3. When you read cases online, their citations are most often to reporters; thus, understanding reporters is important even when researching using exclusively online sources.

Because reporters publish opinions chronologically, researchers need a topical index to locate relevant cases in their jurisdiction. A *digest* serves this purpose. Online services are increasingly providing similar topical indexes to assist with locating cases.

F. Updating with Citators

After finding statutes, cases, and other authorities that address a research topic, you must ensure that these authorities represent the current law. This step is performed using *citators*. The process of using citators to ensure that authorities are still respected is called *updating*. Almost all updating takes place online through competing services: Westlaw offers KeyCite and LexisNexis offers Shepard's. Entering a case citation in either KeyCite or Shepard's will produce a list of authorities that have mentioned that case, along with indications of whether the authorities agreed with it or not. By reviewing the list, you can learn whether a case has been reversed, overruled, distinguished, or followed extensively.

Because citators provide lists of authorities, they are also effective research tools. Entering the citation for one relevant case can quickly produce a list of other cases that may be relevant because they relied on a case you know is relevant.

G. Finishing Research

The goal of research is to solve a client's problem. If you immediately find a primary authority that perfectly answers the client's question, your research may be over. Most research projects, however, do not have a clear answer. You will have to collect bits and pieces of answers in order to construct a solution that meets your client's goals. When there is no clear answer, it can be difficult to know when to stop researching. There are two checkpoints for knowing that research is nearing an end.

First, make an outline of your answer to the client's problems. When there are no analytical holes in the outline, you are likely finished researching. Second, in reviewing secondary sources, statutes, administrative law, and judicial opinions, and then updating relevant authorities, it is likely that you will begin to see the same authorities appear repeatedly. This failure to find new authorities is an excellent sign that your research has been thorough and you should stop looking for additional authorities.

H. Modifying the Process

The basic research process should be customized for each research project. Consider whether you need to follow all seven steps, and if so, in what order. If you are unfamiliar with an area of law, you should follow each step of the process in the order indicated. Beginning with secondary sources will provide both context for the issues you must research and citations to relevant primary authority. As you gain experience in researching legal questions, you may choose to modify the process. For example, if you know that a situation is controlled by a statute, you may choose to begin with that step. Or if you know of a case that is on point, you may decide to update it immediately to find additional cases on the same point. Research strategies are discussed in more detail in Chapter 10.

V. Researching the Law—Organization of This Text

Chapter 2 of this book explains fundamental search techniques for both print and online research. The remaining chapters explain in depth each step of the research process.[4] Chapter 3 covers the California court system and judicial opinions, including how to find cases using digests and online topical searching. Case research is covered first because most legal research will include finding and reading cases, even when other primary authority is on point. Chapter 4 addresses the California Constitution, which is the highest legal authority in the state. Chapter 5 describes researching statutes, and Chapter 6 discusses legislative history research. Chapter 7 addresses administrative law.

After this focus on primary authority, Chapter 8 explains how to update legal authority using Shepard's and KeyCite. Chapter 9 covers secondary sources, the frequent starting point for research in an unfamiliar area of law. The discussion of secondary sources is delayed to emphasize their subordinate position relative to primary authority. Chapter 10 discusses research strategies as well as how to organize your research. You may prefer to skim that chapter now and refer to it frequently, even though a number of references in it will not become clear until you have read the intervening chapters.

Chapter 11 provides an overview of the conventions lawyers follow in citing legal authority in their documents. In addition to discussing California citations under the *California Style Manual*,[5] this chapter introduces the two national citation manuals, the *ALWD Citation Manual: A Professional System of Citation*[6] and *The Bluebook:*

---

4. Law students using this book in a research class will most likely cover the chapters in a different order, reflecting the research strategies needed to complement their other coursework.

5. Edward W. Jessen, *California Style Manual* (4th ed., West 2000).

6. ALWD & Darby Dickerson, *ALWD Citation Manual* (3d ed., Aspen Publishers 2006) ("*ALWD Manual*"). Most citations in this book conform to the *ALWD Manual*.

A Uniform System of Citation.[7] At the end of the book is a selected bibliography of texts on legal research and analysis. The general research texts tend to concentrate on federal resources, supplementing this book's brief introduction to those resources.

---

7. *The Bluebook: A Uniform System of Citation* (The Columbia Law Review et al. eds., 18th ed., The Harvard Law Review Assn. 2005) (*"Bluebook"*).

Chapter 2

Legal Research Techniques

Legal research uses print sources, government and law library websites, and online providers like LexisNexis and Westlaw. While each resource is slightly different, some basic research techniques are shared in common. This chapter covers the basic techniques for using print and online legal resources. Researchers experienced in either print or online resources will find here a helpful review. Those with less experience in one type of resource will need to consider these techniques carefully, as later chapters assume familiarity with them.

I. Print Research Techniques

Today, fewer researchers approach legal problems with a firm foundation in print research techniques. In large part, this is because so much information is available online, which has decreased the demand for print sources among college students and professionals. In legal research, however, not all material is available online. Even when sources are available both online and in print, print sources are sometimes more efficient to use. The efficiency may be simply because the sources are free in a library. More often, the efficiency results from the way the resources are organized.

A. Finding a Legal Source by Citation

Retrieving a document in a print source is easy when you have its citation. Simply find the relevant book and turn to the portion indicated by the citation. The citation may be to a particular volume and page (e.g., for a judicial opinion), a title and section (e.g., for a statute), or a paragraph or section number (e.g., a legal encyclopedia). Example citations are listed below.

Example judicial opinion:	*People v. Davis*, 18 Cal. 4th 712 (1998).
Example statute:	Cal. Penal Code Ann. § 451 (West 2006).
Example encyclopedia:	18A Cal. Jur. 3d *Criminal Law: Crimes Against Property* § 39 (2001).

B. Table-of-Contents Searching

Most print sources begin with a table of contents. One way to search these sources is to skim the table of contents for your research terms. The table of contents will refer to relevant pages, section numbers, or paragraph numbers, depending on how that source is organized.

Because a table of contents lists the headings used in that volume, it provides an analytical overview of the topics covered. Skimming the table of contents of an encyclopedia can show how lawyers typically organize concepts in a particular area of law. Reviewing a table of contents for a statutory provision can provide context for the analysis of a single statute. Thus, you can use the table of contents both to get an overview of the law and to find specific portions of the volume that may contain helpful information.

C. Topic Searching with a Print Index

The index is another frequent starting point in print resources. Using the research terms you generated based on the client's problem, search the index for references to particular pages or sections of the volume. Often, it is wise to spend several minutes in the index looking for a number of research terms. This technique ensures that you begin your research in the most helpful part of the volume, not just the part you encountered first.

It is common for an index to contain cross-references to other entries. Sometimes cross-references can be confusing as to whether they refer to different subheadings or to different main headings. Take a few moments to learn the cross-reference signals of a new book, as they vary among resources.

In multi-volume series, the index is likely to be located in the last volume. Separate indexes may be provided for each volume or for each legal topic. In a digest, for example, the "Analysis" outline at the beginning of a topic can provide context for the concepts covered and suggest particular portions of the topic that may lead to relevant cases.

D. Pocket Parts and Supplements

Many print sources are updated using *pocket parts*. These are extra pages sent by the publisher to be inserted in the back cover of a particular volume. Pocket parts often contain the most recent material available in print, so it is important to check any volume used in research to see whether it has a pocket part. If a pocket part becomes too large to fit in the back of a volume, it will be published as a softbound supplement and shelved next to the volume.

In addition to updates to single volumes, a softbound supplement may exist for an entire series of books. This supplement will likely be shelved at the end of the series. It will contain the most up-to-date information available in print.

II. Online Research Techniques

Lawyers often find online research necessary for conducting efficient and cost-effective legal research. Unlike other online research, however, legal research requires a high level of precision, both in deciding where to search and in constructing searches. This part begins with basic information for conducting legal research online. This introduction will be essential for researchers with less online experience, while providing a quick review for researchers savvy about online techniques. The chapter then delves into more advanced search techniques.

Web addresses for California primary authority are listed in Table 2-1. Some of the more common commercial providers of online legal sources are listed in Table 2-2. In addition to these sources, many legal researchers use "gateway" sites that link to a variety of online resources. Two university-provided gateway sites are Cornell University Law School's Legal Information Institute, at www.law.cornell.edu, and Washburn University School of Law's WashLaw, at www.washlaw.edu.

Table 2-1. Selected Government Websites for California Primary Authority

Type of Authority	Web Address
California Constitution	www.leginfo.ca.gov/const.html
California Statutes	www.leginfo.ca.gov/calaw.html
California Regulations	www.oal.ca.gov (click on "Cal. Code Regs")
California Appellate Opinions	www.courtinfo.ca.gov/opinions

Table 2-2. Selected Websites for Commercial Providers

Provider	Web Address
FindLaw	www.findlaw.com
LexisNexis	www.lexisnexis.com
Loislaw	www.loislaw.com
VersusLaw	www.versuslaw.com
Westlaw	www.westlaw.com

If the information you need is available for free on one of the government or university sites, think carefully before using a costly commercial provider. Sometimes a commercial provider's extensive database or sophisticated search engine will make the cost worthwhile, but you need to consider the costs and efficiencies involved in every search.

A. Finding a Legal Source by Citation

When working online, retrieving a document is as simple as typing the citation into a designated box on the proper screen. Note that online services typically use the print citation to identify particular documents. In other words, to retrieve a case from LexisNexis, you will enter the volume and page of the print reporter. Most online providers list accepted citation formats, which vary from one online site to another.

B. Table-of-Contents Searching

An increasing number of online sources provide tables of contents. As in print research, the advantages to skimming an online table of contents are (1) seeing how various issues and topics are related in that area of law and (2) finding relevant portions of the document or database.

An online table of contents works just like a table of contents in print, except that the initial page will list only major headings. Subheadings may be accessed by clicking a "plus" symbol next to one of the headings. For example, in a dispute over whether an injury that occurred at work is covered by California's workers' compensation laws, you could open the table of contents for California statutes and scan the list until you found the "Labor Code." Clicking on the plus symbol before that code would bring up the major divisions of that code, including Division 4 "Workers' Compensation and Insurance." Subsequent clicks would lead to the division's parts, then chapters, and finally individual statutes.

C. Topic Searching Online

Sophisticated online search engines and services have tools for topic searching. The most user-friendly of these tools allow the researcher to begin with a list of broad areas of law and narrow the topic by clicking through successive lists. On Westlaw, this topic searching tool is called "KeySearch," which is accessed through the

"Key Numbers" link at the top of any screen. Topic searching on Lex-isNexis uses the tool "Search by Topic," available from the "Search" screen.

In either service, you have the option of entering terms into a search box or clicking through lists of topics. To continue the workers' compensation example above, on Westlaw's KeySearch, you could enter the term "workers' compensation" in the search box. The search results would be the topics in KeySearch that contain that term. Alternatively, on either service you could click through successive layers of topics, moving from the general to the specific. Following this approach, you may select the broad topic "Employment Law," then narrow the topic to "Workers' Compensation," and finally choose "Injuries Covered." Under either approach, the final screen requires you to select a jurisdiction, such as California state cases, before running the search.

D. Terms-and-Connectors Searching

One of the most common techniques for searching online is with "terms and connectors." These searches use connecting symbols to dictate where search terms should be in relation to each other in the documents retrieved. An outline of the steps to constructing an effective search is provided in Table 2-3.

Table 2-3. Outline for Constructing Terms-and-Connectors Searches

1. Generate search terms, then modify them with expanders and placeholders.
2. Add connectors.
3. Choose the appropriate sources or databases to search.
4. Use relevant segments or fields to restrict the search by date, court, judge, or other option.
5. Refine the search based on the results.

1. Generate Search Terms

Generate a comprehensive list of search terms, following the suggestions in Chapter 1. This step is critically important in online research, given the literal nature of search engines. If the author of a particular document does not use the exact term you are searching for, that document will not appear in your results.

Next, modify the search terms with expanders and placeholders so that a search will find variations of your words. The exclamation point expands words beyond a common root. For example, *employ!* will find employee, employer, employed, employs, employing, etc. The asterisk serves as a placeholder for an individual letter. Up to three asterisks can be used in a single term. This symbol is helpful when you are not sure which form of the word is used, or when you are not sure of the spelling of a word. For example, the search term *dr*nk* will find drink, drank, and drunk. Placeholders are preferable to the expander in some instances. Using an expander on *trad!* with hopes of finding *trade, trading, trades*, etc. will also produce results that include *traditional*. A better search term may be *trad****.

2. Add Connectors

Connectors determine where search terms will be placed in relation to one another in targeted documents. Effective use of connectors is critical in finding relevant authority. Even minimally sophisticated combinations of parentheses and the various connectors can make your searches much more effective. Table 2-4 summarizes the most common connectors used on LexisNexis and Westlaw.

Most connectors are the same for the two services. However, two differences can cause some confusion. On LexisNexis, searching alternative terms requires the use of the connector "or." On Westlaw, a blank space is interpreted as "or," although typing in that connector will produce the same result. The second difference concerns phrases or terms of art. LexisNexis reads a blank as joining words in a phrase.

Table 2-4. Connectors and Commands

Goal	LexisNexis	Westlaw
Find alternative terms anywhere in the document	or	or blank space
Find both terms anywhere in the document	and &	and &
Find both terms within a particular distance from each other	/p = in 1 paragraph /s = in 1 sentence /n = within n words	/p = in 1 paragraph /s = in 1 sentence /n = within n words
Find terms used as a phrase	leave a blank space between each word of the phrase	put the phrase in quotation marks
Control the hierarchy of searching	parentheses	parentheses
Exclude terms	and not	but not %
Extend the end of a term	!	!
Hold the place of letters in a term	*	*

Table 2-5. Example Queries

Goal	LexisNexis Query	Westlaw Query
Search for alternative terms	spouse or wife or husband	spouse wife husband
Search for the phrase "negligent infliction of emotional distress"	negligent infliction of emotional distress	"negligent infliction of emotional distress"

By contrast, to search a phrase on Westlaw, the terms must be enclosed in quotation marks. Examples are shown in Table 2-5.

In both LexisNexis and Westlaw, parentheses are used to refine terms-and-connectors searches. Note the following example: *(covenant or contract) /p (noncompetition or "restraint of trade") /p employ!* This search will look for paragraphs that contain either of the terms (covenant or contract), either of the terms (noncompetition or "restraint of trade"), and variations of the terms employ, employee, employer, employment, etc. Without the parentheses, the search may look for either covenant or contract within the same paragraph as noncompetition, and so on.

3. Choose Sources or Databases

Terms-and-connectors searches are typically conducted in the full text of documents to look for exact matches. Thus, to begin searching in a service with multiple databases, you must choose which subset of that provider's resources to search. Your research will be more efficient if you restrict each search to the smallest subset of databases that will contain the documents needed. In addition, searches in the smaller subsets are typically less expensive than searches in vast databases.

LexisNexis and Westlaw divide their resources into subsets by type of document, topic, and jurisdiction. In LexisNexis, these groups are simply called "sources." In Westlaw, information is grouped into "databases." Both LexisNexis and Westlaw have directories to allow you to browse among the sources and databases that are available for research. Clicking on the "i" next to the name of a source or database will provide information about its scope. Note that the list of sources or databases shown on a particular page may not include all that are available. On LexisNexis, you may need to click on "View more sources." On Westlaw, you may need to add more databases to those shown on a particular tab.

4. Restrict the Search with "Segments" and "Fields"

With terms-and-connectors searching, both LexisNexis and Westlaw allow you to search specific parts of documents, such as the date, author, or court. On LexisNexis, these specific parts are called document *segments*; on Westlaw, they are called *fields*. These options can be applied through drop-down menus. A segment or field term is added to the basic search with an appropriate connector.

Two examples demonstrate the usefulness of segment and field searching. First, in conducting a full-text search, you can ensure that the results directly address your topic by searching the syllabi or synopses of the documents. Because this segment or field summarizes the contents of the document, your terms will appear there only if they are the focus of the document. Thus, the search will weed out documents where your terms are mentioned only in passing or in a footnote. Second, if you know the author of a relevant opinion or article, you can search for her name in the appropriate segment or field, eliminating documents where the person is referred to only tangentially.

5. Refine the Search with "Focus" and "Locate"

With a query of terms and connectors, a search may result in a reasonable number of highly relevant documents, or no documents, or more than 1,000 documents. In the latter two instances, refining the search is necessary. When a search produces no results, use broader connectors (e.g., search for terms in the same paragraph rather than in the same sentence), use more general terms, or use a larger set of sources or a larger database. When a search produces a long list of results, skim them to see whether they are on point. If the results seem irrelevant, modify or edit the search query by using more specific terms, more restrictive connectors, or a smaller set of sources or databases.

The "Focus" feature on LexisNexis and the "Locate" feature on Westlaw can be used to narrow results further. These features allow a researcher to construct a new search within a prior search, and produce a more refined subset of the initial search results. These features can be very cost efficient because they do not result in the additional charges of a new search. Indeed, a good strategy may be to create a broader initial search than you otherwise might and plan to conduct a series of restricting searches on the results.

6. Example Terms-and-Connectors Search

Continuing the example from Chapter 1, the following Westlaw search uses the tools described above: "negligent infliction of emotional distress" & da(aft 1990). The search will look for the phrase "negligent infliction of emotional distress" in documents published after 1990. After reviewing some of the documents returned in the search, you may decide to refine the search by using the "Locate" feature to restrict to documents containing the words spouse, husband, or wife. If the results are still not sufficiently focused on your topic, consider adding narrower terms.

E. Natural-Language Searching

Natural-language search engines allow searches that use a simple question or phrase, as opposed to an arcane series of terms and connectors. These search engines lack the precision of terms-and-connectors searching but allow you to construct a search more quickly and intuitively. A natural-language search for the project in Chapter 1 is "When is a driver liable to a bystander spouse under negligent infliction of emotional distress?"

Natural-language search engines are designed to produce a list of results and to rank the value of the results. Natural-language searching can seem positive after the frustration of terms-and-connectors searches that return no results, but several caveats are important. On general purpose sites like Google, some hits appear first in result lists simply because sponsors pay for this privilege. Sometimes the best hit from your perspective will be the search engine's fifteenth result, so skimming through the results is always very important.

Furthermore, natural-language searching can produce lists of documents that are not very relevant to your research. This result may mean that no better matches exist or that the search was not crafted well enough. When conducting the search on the Internet, poor results may mean that the particular search engine did not scan the portion of the Internet that contains the needed documents. On Lexis-Nexis and Westlaw, the natural-language programs are set to retrieve a particular number of results. Often that number is 20 or 100, though you can change the default. The fact that the computer returned 100 documents does not mean that those 100 documents are all relevant.

While natural-language searching can be very helpful to the novice online researcher, skilled terms-and-connectors searching will almost always be more powerful and accurate. Law students should take advantage of their unfettered access to LexisNexis and Westlaw by extensively practicing terms-and-connectors searching. Practitioners can take advantage of free training provided by the commercial providers.

F. Moving through Online Documents

In most online services, you can move through the document by scrolling through pages or by clicking through search terms. If the search term feature is not available, try using the "Find" feature on your web browser. Some services allow for book browsing, so that you can see the previous or next page of a set of documents. Reviewing nearby documents through book browsing can help provide context to the original document you were viewing.

G. Printing, Downloading, or Emailing Results

Both LexisNexis and Westlaw allow you to download or email documents as opposed to printing them. These options are effective early in a research project because they allow you to skim quickly to the point where your terms appear using the "Find" function. Moreover, now that most word processors allow highlighting and in-line annotating, you may choose to read and organize your research documents entirely on your computer. However, many researchers still find it easier to read documents carefully on paper as opposed to the computer screen.

Table 2-6. Example Notes for Online Searching

Date of Search: January 5, 2008

Issue: Whether a driver is liable to a bystander spouse under negligent infliction of emotional distress in California

Online Site or Service: LexisNexis

Sources: California state cases (short name: CACTS)

Search Terms: negligent infliction of emotional distress; bystander; spouse; wife; husband; driver

Date Restriction: Last 10 years

Search: negligent infliction of emotional distress & (spouse or wife or husband)

Locate: driver; bystander

Results: [Either list your results here or print a cite list to attach to your notes.]

H. Keeping Track

Those researchers new to online legal searching may benefit from completing the chart in Table 2-6 before beginning a search. Even experienced researchers should keep notes containing the dates searched, the searches performed, and the search results. These notes will help you stay on track and avoid duplicating research on a later date. Notes will also indicate the time period that needs to be updated as you near your project deadline.

Online services provide lists of past searches and results, and you should form the habit of printing or saving them. On LexisNexis, click "History." On Westlaw, click "Research Trail."

.

Chapter 3

Judicial Opinions

Courts write judicial opinions—informally called cases—to explain their decisions in litigated disputes. Cases are published in rough chronological order in books called *reporters*. Some reporters include only cases decided by a certain court, for example, the California Supreme Court. Other reporters include cases from courts within a specific geographic region, for example, the western United States.[1] Reporters are fundamental tools of legal research, regardless of whether a researcher is using print or online sources, because cases are cited to print reporters, even by online services.

This chapter begins with an overview of court systems in California and at the federal level. Then it explains reporters and the features added to opinions when they are published in reporters. Next the chapter discusses how to use digests and online resources to find cases in conducting legal research. The chapter ends with suggestions for reading cases effectively.

I. Court Systems

The basic court structure includes a trial court, an intermediate court of appeals, and an ultimate appellate court, often called the

---

1. Still other reporters publish only those cases that deal with a certain topic, such as bankruptcy, media law, or rules of civil and criminal procedure.

"supreme" court.[2] These courts exist at both the state and federal levels.[3]

A. California Courts

The trial courts of California are called *superior courts*. There are 58 superior courts, one for each of the state's 58 counties. Most counties have multiple court locations, so there are more than 450 trial court locations around the state. Most of the cases in the state system begin in a superior court. These courts hear cases concerning civil, criminal, family, probate, and juvenile matters.[4]

The state's intermediate courts are called *courts of appeal*. The state is divided into six districts. The headquarters of the six districts are provided in Table 3-1. The California Courts of Appeal have appellate jurisdiction over cases decided by the superior courts and by certain administrative agencies. They have original jurisdiction in a few areas, such as habeas corpus. Cases before the courts of appeal are decided by panels composed of three justices.[5] Only a small percent-

---

2. The following discussion omits tribal courts in California. Information is available online for a number of tribal courts. Links are available from the National Indian Law Library, at http://narf.org/nill (click on "Tribal Law Gateway"); the Tribal Court Clearinghouse, at www.tribal-institute.org; California Indian Legal Services, at www.calindian.org; and the California Indian Law Association, at www.calindianlaw.org.

3. Not all states have the three-tier court system of California and the federal judiciary; some do not have an intermediate appellate court. Moreover, in some state systems the highest court is not called the "supreme" court. In New York, for example, the "Court of Appeals" is the highest court.

4. Prior to 1998, California trial courts were divided into superior and municipal courts. Following a constitutional amendment, trial courts were able to unify into superior courts that hear all types of cases. Each of the 58 counties has now moved to the unified system.

5. Jurists on most intermediate appellate courts are called "judges," but California uses the term "justices."

Table 3-1. Districts of the California Courts of Appeal

District	Headquarters
First Appellate District*	San Francisco
Second Appellate District*	Los Angeles
Third Appellate District	Sacramento
Fourth Appellate District*	San Diego
Fifth Appellate District	Fresno
Sixth Appellate District	San Jose

* These three districts are subdivided into divisions.

age of the decisions by California's intermediate appellate courts are published.

California's highest court is the California Supreme Court. This court is located in San Francisco, although it regularly hears cases in Los Angeles and Sacramento, too. The California Supreme Court has seven justices. It has discretion to review cases decided by the courts of appeal, and it exercises that discretion to hear only cases involving significant questions of law or uniform application of the law. This court must, however, hear cases involving the death penalty. These cases are appealed directly from the superior courts to the California Supreme Court.

The California courts' website at www.courtinfo.ca.gov contains a wealth of information about the courts, their jurisdiction, their locations, the dockets, and much more.

B. Federal Courts

In the federal judicial system, the trial courts are called United States District Courts. There are ninety-four district courts in the federal system, with each district drawn from a particular state. California is divided into four federal districts: northern, central, southern, and eastern. A state with a relatively small population may not be subdivided into smaller geographic regions. The entire state of Oregon, for example, makes up the federal District of Oregon.

The federal system's intermediate appellate courts are called United States Courts of Appeals. The country is divided into thirteen federal circuits.[6] California is in the Ninth Circuit, meaning that cases from the United States District Courts located in California are appealed to the United States Court of Appeals for the Ninth Circuit. This circuit encompasses Alaska, Arizona, California, Hawaii, Idaho, Montana, Nevada, Oregon, and Washington, as well as Guam and the Northern Mariana Islands.

The highest court in the federal system is the United States Supreme Court. It decides cases concerning the United States Constitution and federal statutes. This court does not have the final say on matters of purely state law; that authority rests with the highest court of each state. Parties who wish to have the U.S. Supreme Court hear their case must file a petition for *certiorari*, as the court has discretion over which cases it hears.

The website for the federal judiciary contains maps, court addresses, explanations of jurisdiction, and other helpful information. The address is www.uscourts.gov.

II. Reporters

A. Reporters for California Cases

Under the California Constitution, all opinions issued by the California Supreme Court must be published. The official reporter for these cases is *California Reports*. California Court of Appeal opinions are published in a separate official reporter called *California Appellate Reports*. Only some court of appeal cases are published. Opinions that are not published in *California Appellate Reports* are con-

---

6. A map showing the federal circuits is available at www.uscourts.gov/courtlinks.

sidered "unpublished" and may not be cited or used in any manner.[7] Cases from state trial courts in California are not published and therefore cannot be cited or used; in fact, few states publish opinions at the trial court level. Unpublished opinions may be obtained directly from the court that decided the case.

As noted, *California Reports* and *California Appellate Reports* are the official reporters for California appellate cases. Cases from these courts are also reported in two commercially produced, unofficial reporters called *Pacific Reporter* and *West's California Reporter*, both published by West. In 1960, West stopped publishing California Court of Appeal cases in *Pacific Reporter* when it began publishing *West's California Reporter*, which publishes cases from both levels of appellate courts. California Supreme Court cases are also still published in *Pacific Reporter*. While the text of the court's opinion is the same in the official and unofficial reporters, the appearance, pagination, and editorial additions are different. The various reporters for California's appellate cases are summarized in Table 3-2.

Commercial reporters often combine several courts' opinions under a single title. *Pacific Reporter* publishes cases from the courts of the following fifteen states: Alaska, Arizona, California, Colorado, Hawaii, Idaho, Kansas, Montana, Nevada, New Mexico, Oklahoma, California, Utah, Washington, and Wyoming.[8] *Pacific Reporter* in-

---

7. Cal. R. Ct. 8.1115. There are two other instances when cases cannot be cited or quoted. The first instance is a Court of Appeal case that has been accepted for review by the Supreme Court or in which the Supreme Court has reached a decision. The second instance is when the Supreme Court orders a Court of Appeal case "depublished" because one of the parties has asked for depublication or the Supreme Court disagrees with the reasoning of the case. Depublished cases can often be found in *West's California Reporter* and *Pacific Reporter*, and on Westlaw or LexisNexis, but these cases will not appear in the bound official reporter. Because these cases were assigned pages in the advance sheet, the official reporter pages will be blank with a notice that the case has been depublished. The depublication system is governed by Cal. R. Ct. 8.1125.

8. If a state does not publish its own reporter, the regional reporter may be the official reporter. For example, the official reporter of Alaska cases is *Pacific Reporter*. The publisher, West, also publishes an offprint of *Pacific Re-*

Table 3-2. Reporters for California Appellate Cases*

Court	Reporter Name	Abbreviation
California Supreme Court	*California Reports* (official)	Cal., Cal. 2d, Cal. 3d, Cal. 4th
	Pacific Reporter	P., P.2d, P.3d
	West's California Reporter	Cal. Rptr., Cal. Rptr. 2d, Cal. Rptr. 3d
California Courts of Appeal	*California Appellate Reports* (official)	Cal. App., Cal. App. 2d, Cal. App. 3d, Cal. App. 4th
	Pacific Reporter (through 1959)	P., P.2d, P.3d
	West's California Reporter (since 1960)	Cal. Rptr., Cal. Rptr. 2d, Cal. Rptr. 3d

* Some opinions of the Superior Court Appellate Division are published in a separate section of *California Appellate Reports*.

cludes cases from the intermediate and highest appellate courts of most of these states. Other regional reporters are *North Eastern Reporter*, *Atlantic Reporter*, *South Eastern Reporter*, *Southern Reporter*, *South Western Reporter*, and *North Western Reporter*. All of these regional reporters are published by West. Because publishers decide which states to group together in regional reporters, these groupings have no legal impact. Moreover, the coverage of each regional reporter is not the same as the composition of the federal circuits.

Reporters are published in *series*. Cases currently being published in *California Reports* and *California Appellate Reports* are appearing in the fourth series. *Pacific Reporter* is in its third series. To find a case in a reporter with multiple series, you must know which series the

---

porter that contains only Alaska cases. It is called *Alaska Reporter*. The appearance, pagination, and editorial aids are exactly like those in *Pacific Reporter*, but the volumes contain only those pages that report cases from Alaska courts.

case was reported in. This information is included in the citation to the case, as explained below.

Cases are also published electronically. The opinions of courts in California and the rest of the United States can be found on two fee-based services, Westlaw and LexisNexis.[9] Court opinions can also be found on FindLaw, which is owned by West. Finally, the opinions of California courts are published on the official website of the courts, www.courtinfo.ca.gov. This website is linked to a site maintained by LexisNexis, the publisher of the official reporters for California cases. Unlike the general LexisNexis website, this website is free. It is maintained primarily for citizens of California who are doing their own research, not for lawyers.

1. Citing California Cases

A citation to a California case requires the name of the parties, the volume and abbreviation for the reporter, the initial page of the case, and the date.[10] *California Reports* is abbreviated as "Cal." The case *People v. Davis*, 18 Cal. 4th 712 (1998), can be found in volume 18 of the fourth series of *California Reports*, starting on page 712. The case was decided in 1998. The abbreviation for *California Appellate Reports* is "Cal. App." The case *People v. Wise*, 25 Cal. App. 4th 339 (1st Dist. 1994) was published in volume 25 of the fourth series of *California Appellate Reports*, beginning on page 339. It was decided in 1994 by the Court of Appeal for the First District.

In California, all documents submitted to a California court must cite to the official reporter; citation to additional reporters is optional.[11] For documents that are not going to be submitted to a Cal-

---

9. Both services are available to law students through their school's subscription. While the students are not charged, the schools pay fees that are negotiated based on prior usage or enrollment.

10. The following citations adhere to the style of the *ALWD Citation Manual*. For format adhering to the *California Style Manual* or the *Bluebook*, see Chapter 11.

11. Cal. R. Ct. 3.1113(c).

ifornia court, lawyers usually follow the custom of their firm or office. Often that customary reporter will be the West regional reporter listed above. Especially when writing a memo for a firm outside of California, you would likely cite the California cases mentioned above to *Pacific Reporter* or *West's California Reporter*. To indicate which state's courts decided cases cited to a regional reporter, include an abbreviation at the beginning of the date parenthetical.

> EXAMPLES: *People v. Davis*, 958 P.2d 1083 (Cal. 1998).
>
> *State v. Warner*, 696 P.2d 1052 (Or. 1985).

Sometimes you will want to include citations to all reporters that have published an opinion. Multiple citations that refer to the same case in different reporters are called *parallel citations*.

> EXAMPLES: *People v. Davis*, 18 Cal. 4th 712, 958 P.2d 1083, 76
> Cal. Rptr. 2d 770 (1998).
>
> *State v. Warner*, 298 Or. 640, 696 P.2d 1052 (1985).

Note that the California Supreme Court case has three parallel citations, whereas the Oregon case has only two parallel citations. Because California Courts of Appeal cases are no longer published in *Pacific Reporter*, a California Court of Appeal case will have only two parallel citations.

2. Features of a Reported Case

The following discussion relates to cases published in *West's California Reporter* or *Pacific Reporter*. Both of these reporters are published by the same publisher; therefore, this discussion of the features of a reported case applies to all of the unofficially reported California cases. Knowing how West organizes its cases will also provide you with the tools to understand what you see in a case published by a different publisher or available online.

A case printed in a reporter contains the exact language of the court's opinion. Additionally, the publisher adds supplemental information intended to aid researchers in learning about the case, locating the relevant parts of the case, and finding similar cases. Some of

Figure 3-3. Case Excerpt
People v. Davis, 76 Cal. Rptr. 2d 770 (1998)

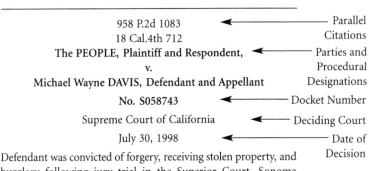

958 P.2d 1083 ◄——————— Parallel
18 Cal.4th 712 Citations

The PEOPLE, Plaintiff and Respondent, ◄——— Parties and
v. Procedural
Michael Wayne DAVIS, Defendant and Appellant Designations

No. S058743 ◄——————— Docket Number

Supreme Court of California ◄——— Deciding Court

July 30, 1998 ◄——————— Date of
Decision

Defendant was convicted of forgery, receiving stolen property, and
burglary following jury trial in the Superior Court, Sonoma
County, No. SCR22933, George L. Nelson, Retired Judge of the
Justice Court, sitting by assignment. Defendant appealed, and The
Court of Appeal affirmed. The Supreme Court granted review, su-
perseding the opinion of the Court of Appeal, and held in an opin- ◄— Synopsis
ion by George, C.J., that placing a forged check in a chute in the
walk-up window of a check-cashing facility, or inserting a stolen
ATM card into an ATM, is not an "entry" for purposes of the burglary statute, disapproving *People v. Ravenscroft*, 198 Cal.App.3d
639, 243 Cal.Rptr. 827.

Judgment of Court of Appeal affirmed in part, reversed in part. ◄— Disposition

Baxter, J., filed a dissenting opinion in which Chin and
Brown, JJ., Joined.

Opinion, 59 Cal.Rptr.2d 584, vacated.

1. Burglary ☞ 9(2) ◄——————— Headnote
   Passing forged check through a chute in a walk-up window of
   a check-cashing facility, or inserting stolen automated teller
   machine (ATM) card into an ATM, is not an "entry" within the
   meaning of the burglary statute; although intended result in
   each instance is larceny, neither act violates occupant's posses-
   sory interest in building as does using a tool to reach into a
   building and remove property; disapproving People v. Ravenscroft, 198 Cal.App.3d 639, 243 Cal.Rptr. 827. West's Ann.Cal.
   Penal Code § 459.

2. Burglary ☞ 2
   Burglary may be committed by using an instrument to enter
   a building, whether that instrument is used solely to effect
   entry, or to accomplish the intended larceny or felony as well.
   West's Ann.Cal.Penal Code § 459.

these research aids are gleaned from the court record of the case while others are written by the publisher's editorial staff. Most reporters will include most of these items, though perhaps in a different order. To best understand the following discussion, refer to a volume of *West's California Reporter*, preferably a volume containing a case you are familiar with. Alternatively, refer to the case excerpt in Figure 3-3 for examples of the concepts explained below.

Parallel citation. The reporter provides the citation for the case in any official or other unofficial reporter in which the case is also printed.

Parties and procedural designations. Most reported cases are from appellate courts. The appealing party is called the *appellant*; the other party is the *respondent*.[12]

Docket number. The docket number is a series of letters and numbers assigned by a court for keeping track of documents pertaining to a particular case.

Deciding court. The opinion gives the full name of the court that decided the case. For cases from the Courts of Appeal, this information includes both the district and, where appropriate, the division.

Date of decision. Each case begins with the date the case was argued and submitted to the court, and the date of the court's decision. For citation purposes, only the year the case was decided is important.

Synopsis. The synopsis is a short summary of the key facts, procedure, legal points, and disposition of the case. Reading a synopsis can quickly tell you whether a case is on point. You cannot rely exclusively on a synopsis and you must never cite it, but it is a very useful research tool.

Disposition. The disposition of the case is the court's decision to affirm, reverse, remand, or vacate the decision below. If the appellate court agrees with only part of the lower court's decision, the appellate court may affirm in part and reverse in part.

---

12. In most jurisdictions, the terms appellant-appellee are used when a party has a right to appeal, while the terms petitioner-respondent apply to parties when the court has discretion to hear the appeal. California uses the term respondent for the non-moving party in both instances.

Headnotes. A headnote is a sentence or short paragraph that sets out a single point of law in a case. Most cases will have several headnotes. The text of each headnote often comes directly from the text of the opinion. But because only the opinion itself is authoritative, do not rely on headnotes in doing research and do not cite them in legal documents. At the beginning of each headnote is a number identifying it in sequence with other headnotes. Within the text of the opinion, the same sequence number will appear in bold print or in brackets at the point in the text supporting the headnote. Using these headnote numbers to find the point of law in the text is a quick way to locate particular points that interest you.

Just after the sequence number, each headnote begins with a word or phrase, a key symbol, and a number. These are *topics* and *key numbers*, which are used in subject indexes to locate other cases that discuss similar points of law. These subject indexes, called *digests*, are discussed later in this chapter.

Headnotes are generally the product of a given reporter's editorial staff, even when the text of the headnote is identical to language used in the opinion. Thus, the number of headnotes—and the text of the headnotes—will differ depending on which publisher's reporter is being used. Because the official and unofficial reporters are published by different publishers, the headnotes in *California Reports* and *California Appellate Reports*, the official reporters, and the headnotes of *West's California Reporter* and *Pacific Reporter* are quite different.

Procedural information. West's California Reporter volumes contain a variety of procedural information. For example, those volumes indicate the court from which the case was appealed, the justices who heard the case, and the justice who wrote the decision. Note that following a justice's name will be "C.J." for the chief justice (or "P.J." for the presiding justice in the Court of Appeal) or "J." for another justice. If a case includes concurring or dissenting opinions, they will be noted in the procedural listings. Also in this section will be the names of the attorneys who argued for each party.

Opinion. In *West's California Reporter*, the actual opinion of the court begins immediately following the name of the justice who wrote the opinion. If the justices who heard the case do not agree on the outcome or the reasons for the outcome, there may be several opinions. The opinion supported by a majority of the justices is called the *majority opinion*. An opinion written to agree with the outcome but not the reasoning of the majority is called a *concurring opinion*. An opinion written by justices who disagree with the outcome supported by the majority of the justices is called a *dissenting opinion*. While only the majority opinion is binding precedent, the other opinions provide valuable insights and may be cited as persuasive authority. If there is no majority on both the outcome and the reasoning, the case will be decided by whichever opinion garners the most support, which is called a *plurality decision*.

Cases decided by the California Supreme Court are heard by all seven of the sitting justices. Cases decided by the California Courts of Appeal are heard by three justices sitting as a *panel* of the full court. A party who does not agree with the decision of the panel may ask for a rehearing *en banc*, meaning that all of the justices on that court would rehear the case.

3. Tables in Reporters

Each volume of *West's California Reporter* contains several helpful tables. Judges and justices serving on the Supreme Court, the Courts of Appeal, and the Superior Courts during the time of the cases reported in each volume are listed in tables at the front of the volume.

An alphabetical listing of all the cases reported in each volume is provided. In *West's California Reporter*, the listing includes cases in which the California Supreme Court has granted or denied petitions for review. The court rarely issues opinions when it grants, denies, or dismisses petitions; instead, it issues a *memorandum* decision that simply records its action on the petition. You can identify these cases by the abbreviation "(Mem.)" following the case name. Most petitions for review by the California Supreme Court are denied; however, denying a petition does not mean that the court agrees with the outcome or analysis in the lower court's opinion.

Following the list of cases, *West's California Reporter* provides a section called Words and Phrases. This list indicates cases in that volume of the reporter that define particular legal terms. At the back of each reporter is a subject index, the Key Number Digest. The topics and key numbers at the beginning of each headnote are included in the index. Searching the index can point you to additional cases that are on point, as addressed later in this chapter.

4. Advance Sheets

The bound volumes of reporters can take months to be published, with official reporters usually taking much longer than commercial reporters. To make cases available in print sooner, publishers supply subscribers with softbound booklets called *advance sheets*. The advance sheets for *West's California Reporter* are published weekly on Fridays. They include cases from the California Supreme Court and the California Courts of Appeal in one booklet.

The pagination used in the advance sheets is the same as will be used in the hardbound volumes; thus, a cite to a case in the advance sheets will still be accurate after the case is published in hardbound volumes. An advance sheet section begins numbering with page one when a new hardbound volume is anticipated.

Each advance sheet contains a table of cases included in that volume as well as a key number index. Additionally, the advance sheets for *West's California Reporter* report modifications to California Published Opinions; monthly updates to California civil and criminal jury instructions; a summary of cases accepted for review by the Supreme Court; a Case History Table; a Cumulative Review, Rehearing and Hearing Table; and Parallel Citation Tables. Advance sheet pages containing these types of materials have page numbers at the bottom of the page to distinguish them from the pages that will be included in the bound reporter volumes, which show the numbers at the top of the page.

5. *Other Sources for Finding California Cases*

To provide access to cases even faster than advance sheets can be published, *slip opinions* are available either from the court that decided the case or online at www.courtinfo.ca.gov/opinions. A slip opinion is the actual document produced by the court, without the editorial enhancements normally added by the publisher. California Supreme Court cases are posted immediately upon filing. These opinions are normally filed at 10:30 a.m. on Mondays and Thursdays. California Court of Appeal opinions are routinely posted within a few hours of filing and may be filed any time during the day. In addition, cases are added daily to both the LexisNexis and Westlaw services, which are often the fastest way to find a new opinion, particularly one from a state other than California (which may not post opinions so quickly).

B. Reporters for Federal Cases

Reporters are also published for cases decided by federal courts. Table 3-4 lists the federal court reporters, along with their citation abbreviations.

Decisions of the United States Supreme Court are reported in *United States Reports* (official); *Supreme Court Reporter* (West); and *United States Supreme Court Reports, Lawyers' Edition* (LexisNexis). Although the official *United States Reports* should be cited if possible,

Table 3-4. Reporters for Federal Court Cases

Court	Reporter Name	Abbreviation
U.S. Supreme Court	*United States Reports* (official)	U.S.
	Supreme Court Reporter	S. Ct.
	United States Supreme Court Reports, Lawyers' Edition	L. Ed., L. Ed. 2d
U.S. Courts of Appeals	*Federal Reporter*	F., F.2d, F.3d
U.S. District Courts	*Federal Supplement*	F. Supp., F. Supp. 2d

that series frequently publishes cases several years after they are decided. Thus, for recent cases, lawyers often cite the *Supreme Court Reporter*. Another source for finding recent cases from the Supreme Court is *United States Law Week*. This service publishes the full text of cases from the Supreme Court and provides summaries of important decisions of state and federal courts.

Cases decided by the federal intermediate appellate courts are published in *Federal Reporter*, now in its third series. Some United States Courts of Appeals cases that were not selected for publication in *Federal Reporter*, and might not be precedential, may be published in a relatively new reporter series, *Federal Appendix*. Selected cases from the United States District Courts, the federal trial courts, are reported in *Federal Supplement* and *Federal Supplement, Second Series*.

Supreme Court opinions are widely available online. The Court's website at www.supremecourtus.gov/opinions/opinions.html includes slip opinions soon after the decisions are rendered. Limited access to court of appeals and district court cases may be available from the individual court's website. An educational site supported by Cornell University also provides federal cases quickly; the address is www.law.cornell.edu/supct. LexisNexis and Westlaw publish federal opinions soon after they are released. Remember that LexisNexis and Westlaw make available "unpublished" opinions. Check court rules to determine the weight each court gives to unpublished opinions before citing one.

III. West Digests

A digest is a multi-volume or online index in which cases are organized by subject. Under each subject, the digest provides one or more headnotes from each case that address that particular subject and a citation to the case. The digest does not reprint the entire case. Digests are important research tools because reporters organize cases chronologically, rather than by subject. The digest serves as a subject index to reporters.

This part of the chapter concentrates on digests published by West because they are the most widely used throughout the country. Much of the information provided here would apply to any other case digest as well.

The digest most often used in California for researching California law is *West's California Digest 2d*. It includes headnotes of cases from state courts in California. Headnotes from cases that originated in California and were later decided by the Ninth Circuit and the United States Supreme Court are indexed here, too. This digest also includes references to opinions of the California attorney general and articles published by California law reviews. An example of entries in *West's California Digest 2d* is given in Figure 3-5.

Some digests index cases from a number of different jurisdictions. For instance, *Pacific Digest* contains headnotes of cases that are reported in *Pacific Reporter*, which were decided by many different state courts. Another digest, *Federal Practice Digest*, provides an index to cases decided by federal trial and appellate courts. West's *Decennial Digest* indexes cases from all United States jurisdictions that are reported in West's national reporter system. Each of these digests is published by West and uses the West topic-key number system. Table 3-6 lists several digests useful in California research.

West's California Digest 2d includes cases from 1950 to the present. Like many other digests, *West's California Digest 2d* is not cumulative, so you must look in the first edition, *West's California Digest*, for headnotes of cases decided between 1850 and 1950. Similarly, *Pacific Digest* publishes bound sets periodically; the most recent includes cases reported in volume 585 of *Pacific Reporter, Second Series* and subsequent volumes. To do thorough research in *West's California Digest*, *Pacific Digest*, and other non-cumulative digests, you may need to consult more than one series. Consider the period of time that is pertinent for your research, and then check the introductory information at the front of each digest to determine whether the digest covers that period.

**Figure 3-5. Excerpts from *West's California Digest 2d*
"Adverse Possession"**

N.D.Cal. 1992. State satisfied elements of adverse possession for disputed park land under California law and, thus, logging company did not own land which it had purported to donate to state for charitable tax deduction, where state's occupation of property in dispute had continued for at least five years, and had been real, adverse to claims of others, and hostile to claims of others; state had marked boundary of park with signs, monuments, and other indicia of property being state park, and logging company had logged trees only up to indicated boundary of park. West's Ann.Cal.C.C.P. §§ 322, 325.

Kamilche Co. v. U.S., 809 F.Supp. 763, reversed 53 F.3d 1059, opinion amended on rehearing 75 F.3d 1391.

Cal. 1981. Elements necessary to establish title by adverse possession are tax payment and open and notorious use or possession that is continuous and uninterrupted, hostile to the true owner and under claim of title. West's Ann.C.C.P. § 325.

Gilardi v. Hallam, 636 P.2d 588, 178 Cal.Rptr. 624, 30 Cal.3d 317.

Cal. 1954. To establish title by adverse possession, claimant must show possession by actual occupancy under circumstances constituting reasonable notice to owner, possession hostile to owner's title, claim to property as his own, either under color of title or claim of right, continuous and uninterrupted possession for five years, and payment of all taxes levied and assessed during period.

Laubisch v. Roberdo, 277 P.2d 9, 43 Cal.2d 702.

Cal.App. 1 Dist. 1990. Elements necessary to establish title by adverse possession are tax payment and open and notorious use or possession that is continuous and uninterrupted, hostile to true owner and under claim of title for five years. West's Ann.Cal.C.C.P. §§ 321–325.

Sevier v. Locher, 272 Cal.Rptr. 287, 222 Cal.App.3d 1082.

Source: *West's California Digest 2d*, volume 1A, page 503. Reprinted with permission of West, a Thomson business.

Table 3-6. Selected Digests

California Digest	Cases from California courts and federal courts in California (and appellate review of those cases)
Pacific Digest	Cases from states included in *Pacific Reporter*
Decennial Digest	Cases from all jurisdictions included in West's national reporter system
Federal Practice Digest	Cases from United States District Courts, United States Courts of Appeals, and the United States Supreme Court (and some topical federal reporters)
United States Supreme Court Digest	Cases from the United States Supreme Court

A. Digest Features

1. Topics and Key Numbers

West digests index cases according to the West system of *topics* and *key numbers*. West assigns a topic and key number to each headnote in a case, based on the legal point that is the focus of the headnote. The West *topic* places the headnote within a broad subject area of the law. Examples of West topics include "Criminal Law," "Health and Environment," and "Zoning and Planning." The *key number* relates to a subtopic within that area of law. An example of a topic-key number for cases dealing with criminal evidence is "Criminal Law 338(1)." The key number 338(1) refers to the subtopic "Evidence-Facts in Issue and Relevance."

"Criminal Law" is a vast topic, containing over 1,000 key numbers on subtopics covering criminal intent, defenses, pleas, trials, and sentencing guidelines. As an example of a much shorter topic, "Products Liability" includes approximately 100 key numbers on subtopics addressing products in general, particular products, and aspects of legal actions such as the burden of proof and the admissibility of evidence.

2. Headnotes

The digest entries under each topic-key number are the actual headnotes found in cases (see Figure 3-3, showing the headnotes in a case). The bulk of each headnote entry is a sentence that summarizes the point of law that is the specific subject of the topic-key number assigned to that headnote. Each case is indexed in the digest under as many topics and key numbers as it had headnotes in the reporter.

In a digest, headnotes are arranged under each topic-key number according to the court that decided the case. Federal cases are listed first, followed by state cases. Within the federal and state systems, cases are listed according to judicial hierarchy: cases from the highest appellate court are listed first, followed by cases of intermediate appellate courts, then trial court cases. In *West's California Digest 2d*, cases from the California Courts of Appeal are organized starting with the first district and continuing through the sixth district in ascending numerical order. Cases from each court are given in reverse chronological order. This order is helpful because recent cases, which are listed first, are more likely to be pertinent to your research.

At the beginning of each headnote is a court abbreviation and date. The abbreviations are explained in tables at the beginning of each digest volume. At the end of the digest headnote are citations to any statutes that are cited in the case. This information is followed by the case citation and any parallel citations.

Although West may have assigned a topic-key number to a particular point of law, a given jurisdiction may not have decided a case on that point. In that instance, no entries will appear under the topic-key number of that jurisdiction's digest. However, the topic-key number system makes it easy to research cases in other jurisdictions using West digests, which may lead to persuasive authorities.

Table 3-7. Outline for Digest Research with
the Descriptive-Word Index

---

1. Find your research terms in the Descriptive-Word Index (and
    its pocket part), which will list topics and key numbers rel-
    evant to those terms.
2. Review each topic and key number in the main volumes of
    the digest.
3. Update each topic and key number by checking the pocket
    parts or volume supplement, the cumulative supplementary
    pamphlets, and the digests contained in the reporter's most
    recent advance sheets.

B. Digest Research

1. Beginning with a Relevant Case

If you begin a research project knowing one case on point, read
the case in a West reporter and identify the headnotes that are relevant to your issue. Note the topic and key number given for each relevant headnote. Select a digest volume containing one of the relevant
topics; within that topic, find the key number given in the related
headnote. Under the key number, all the headnotes of cases with that
topic-key number will be listed. Repeat this step for each relevant
topic-key number in your original case. Remember to update the
search to find the most recent cases on point.

2. Beginning with the Descriptive-Word Index

Most digest research begins with the Descriptive-Word Index, which
translates research terms into the topics and key numbers used by the
digest to index cases. See Table 3-7 for an outline of this process.

To begin, use an organized method of brainstorming to generate
a list of research terms that describe the situation you are analyzing.
Then look up each term in the Descriptive-Word Index (contained in

Figure 3-8. Excerpts from the Descriptive-Word Index in *West's California Digest 2d*

---

45 Cal D 2d-85   ADVERSE

References are to Digest Topic and Key Numbers

ADVERSE POSSESSION-Cont'd
HOSTILE possession, **Adv Poss**
  58–85, 114(1), 115(5), 116(5)
HUSBAND and wife,
  Married women, **Hus & W 69.5**
INDIAN lands, **Indians 22**
INSTRUCTIONS to jury,
  Adv Poss 116
INTERRUPTION of possession, **Adv**
  Poss 46–49
JOINT tenancy, **Joint Ten 9**
JUDGMENT,
  Color of title, **Adv Poss 74**
  Title or right to property,
    Adv Poss 51
JUDICIAL sales,
  Color of title, **Adv Poss 74**
JURY questions, **Adv Poss 115**
  Tenancy in common, **Ten in C 15(11)**

KNOWLEDGE or notice,
  Former owner, **Adv Poss 31**
LANDLORD and tenant, **Land &**
  Ten 66
LAWFUL possession element,
  Adv Poss 26
LEGATEES,
  Hostile character of possession,
    Adv Poss 62(1)
LICENSES,
  Possession after amicable entry,
    Adv Poss 60(2)
LIFE estates. See heading **LIFE ESTATES**
LIMITATIONS,
  Bar,
    Action for recovery of land,
      Adv Poss 106(2)
  Suspension of statute, **Adv Poss 45**

Source: *West's California Digest 2d*. Reprinted with permission of West, a Thomson business.

several volumes at the end of the digest) and write down the topic and key number for each. Record both the topic and the key number; many topics have the same key numbers, so a number alone is not a helpful research tool. Check each volume's pocket part for the most recent information. Figure 3-8 shows an excerpt from the Descriptive-Word Index in *West's California Digest 2d*. Note that some topics are abbreviated in the Descriptive-Word Index. A list of topics and their abbreviations is included at the front of each index volume.

Using the topics and key numbers you recorded from the Descriptive-Word Index, select a digest volume that contains one of the topics. At the beginning of each topic is a list of "Subjects In-

Figure 3-9. Excerpts from *West's California Digest 2d* Analysis for Adverse Possession

---

Analysis

I. NATURE AND REQUISITES, ⊟▥▥ 1–95.

   (A)   ACQUISITION OF RIGHTS BY PRESCRIPTION IN GENERAL, ⊟▥▥ 1–13.

   (B)   ACTUAL POSSESSION, ⊟▥▥ 14–27.

   (C)   VISIBLE AND NOTORIOUS POSSESSION, ⊟▥▥ 28–33.

   (D)   DISTINCT AND EXCLUSIVE POSSESSION, ⊟▥▥ 34–38.

   (E)   DURATION AND CONTINUITY OF POSSESSION, ⊟▥▥ 39–57.

   (F)   HOSTILE CHARACTER OF POSSESSION, ⊟▥▥ 58–85.

   (G)   PAYMENT OF TAXES, ⊟▥▥ 86–95.

II. OPERATION AND EFFECT, ⊟▥▥ 96–109.

   (A)   EXTENT OF POSSESSION, ⊟▥▥ 96–103.

   (B)   TITLE OR RIGHT ACQUIRED, ⊟▥▥ 104–109.

III. PLEADING, ⊟▥▥ 110, 111.

IV. EVIDENCE, ⊟▥▥ 112–114.

V. TRIAL, ⊟▥▥ 115–117.

Source: *West's California Digest 2d*. Reprinted with permission of West, a Thomson business.

cluded" as well as "Subjects Excluded and Covered by Other Topics." These lists will help you decide whether that topic is likely to index cases most relevant to your research. The list of excluded subjects may contain references to other relevant topics found elsewhere in the digest. After these lists is the key number outline of the topic, under the heading "Analysis," as seen in Figure 3-9. Longer topics will contain a short, summary outline and then a detailed outline. Many topics follow a general litigation organization, so that elements, defenses, pleadings, and evidence are discussed in that order. Take a moment to skim the Analysis outline to ensure that you found in the Descriptive-Word Index all the relevant key numbers within that topic.

Next turn to each of the relevant key numbers and carefully review each of the case headnotes listed there. Write down the citation for each case that you decide you need to read. At this point, the cites do not have to be complete or conform to any system of citation. Recording the last name of one party, the volume, reporter, and page number will often be sufficient.

To find more recent topics, key numbers, and case headnotes, check the back of the volume for pocket parts. A softbound volume of updated material may be provided instead, if the material is too thick to fit in a pocket part. These supplements are in turn updated by cumulative supplementary pamphlets, which contain updates for all topics. For same-day currency, you must go to an online database, such as LexisNexis or Westlaw, which are explained below.

Reviewing headnotes and recording possibly relevant case citations is time-consuming but critical work. To analyze a client's situation accurately, you need to read every relevant case; the cost of skipping a key case is high. However, you may be selective in deciding which cases to read first. Additionally, when a topic-key number contains many pages of case headnotes, or when you are working under tight deadlines, you may need to be selective in choosing the cases you are able to read. First, read those cases that are binding authority in your jurisdiction. Within that subset, read the most recent cases. If a headnote includes facts similar to your client's, read that case, too.

3. Beginning with the Topic Analysis

After researching a specific area of law many times, you may be very familiar with the topics under which cases in that area are indexed. If so, you can begin your research using the Analysis outline that appears at the beginning of each relevant topic. Scan the list of key number subtopics, and then review the headnotes under each key number that

Figure 3-10. Excerpt from Words and Phrases
in *West's California Digest 2d*

HOSTILITY

   Cal.App. Dist. 1992. For purposes of establishing adverse possession,
element of "hostility" means that claimant's possession is adverse to
record owner, unaccompanied by any recognition, express or inferable
from circumstances, of right in latter, and not that parties have dispute
as to title during period of possession.—Buic v. Buic, 7 Cal.Rptr.2d 738,
5 Cal.App.4th 1600.—Adv Poss 60(3).

Source: *West's California Digest 2d*. Reprinted with permission of West, a
Thomson business.

appears to be on point. As always, remember to check the pocket parts,
supplementary pamphlets, and reporter advance sheets for more recent cases under the topics and key numbers you are searching.

4. Words and Phrases

   To learn whether a court has defined a term, refer to the Words
and Phrases volumes at the end of the digest. While a dictionary like
Black's Law Dictionary will provide a general definition of a term,
Words and Phrases will direct you to a case that defines the term for
a particular jurisdiction. (See Figure 3-10.) Judicial definitions are especially helpful when an important term in a statute is vague.

5. Table of Cases

   The Table of Cases lists all the cases indexed in a particular digest
series by both the primary plaintiff's name and the primary defendant's name. The table is helpful when you do not know the citation
to a relevant case but do know the name of one or both parties. This
situation may occur (1) because a colleague recommended the case,
(2) because you used it in previous research, or (3) because the only
citation you have is to the official reporter, which does not use West's

topics and key numbers. The Table of Cases provides the full name of the case, the citation for the case, and the relevant topics and key numbers. After consulting the Table of Cases, you could either read the case in a reporter or continue working in the digest using the listed topics and key numbers to find more related cases.

IV. Online Subject Searching

A. LexisNexis and Westlaw

Both Westlaw and LexisNexis offer ways to search for cases by subject. On Westlaw, options include the "Custom Digest" feature for searching by digest topic and key number, and the "KeySearch" feature for searching by subject alone. On LexisNexis, the feature for subject searching is "Search by Topic."

These features on Westlaw and LexisNexis have a number of characteristics in common. First, both systems display breakdowns of topics that resemble the Analysis outline of a print digest. In both systems, you can expand the list of general topics to get more specific subtopics by clicking on a symbol or icon at the left of the general topic listing. This expander feature most commonly consists of a "plus" symbol, although in Westlaw's KeySearch, the expander currently is a file folder. The approach here, as with print digest searching, is to decide where in the larger scheme of legal topics your more specific topic is likely to be located. For example, "Adverse Possession" is its own topic in *West's California Digest 2d*, and that topic will also appear in the Westlaw Custom Digest feature. (See Figure 3-11.) However, in both Westlaw's KeySearch and LexisNexis's Search by Topic features, you would need to start with the larger topic of "Real Property" and use the expanders to find the more specific topic of "Adverse Possession."

The second common feature is that both Westlaw and LexisNexis provide a search box for typing in terms that may lead to a relevant topic. On Westlaw, the box appears in the left frame of the KeySearch screen. On LexisNexis, "Option 1" under "Search by Topic or Head-

Figure 3-11. Westlaw Custom Digest
"Adverse Possession"

Source: Westlaw. Reprinted with permission of West, a Thomson business.

note" is a similar search box. Typing in "adverse possession" will lead to a list of relevant topics and subtopics. (See Figure 3-12.)

Regardless of the feature you use, both systems eventually take you to a screen where you must select the jurisdiction for your search and the type of documents you wish to retrieve (e.g., state cases, federal cases, secondary sources). The screen provides a search box where you have the option of entering either a terms-and-connectors search or a natural-language search. Figure 3-13 shows the KeySearch search page on Westlaw.

Ultimately, both Westlaw and LexisNexis will provide a list of cases (KeySearch and Search by Topic) or headnotes (Custom Digest) that relate to your topic. The headnotes on Westlaw will be the same as those in *West's California Digest 2d*, while the headnotes on LexisNexis will be those that appear in the print official reporters, *California Reports* and *California Appellate Reports*, as well as on LexisNexis ver-

Figure 3-12. LexisNexis Search by Topic Feature

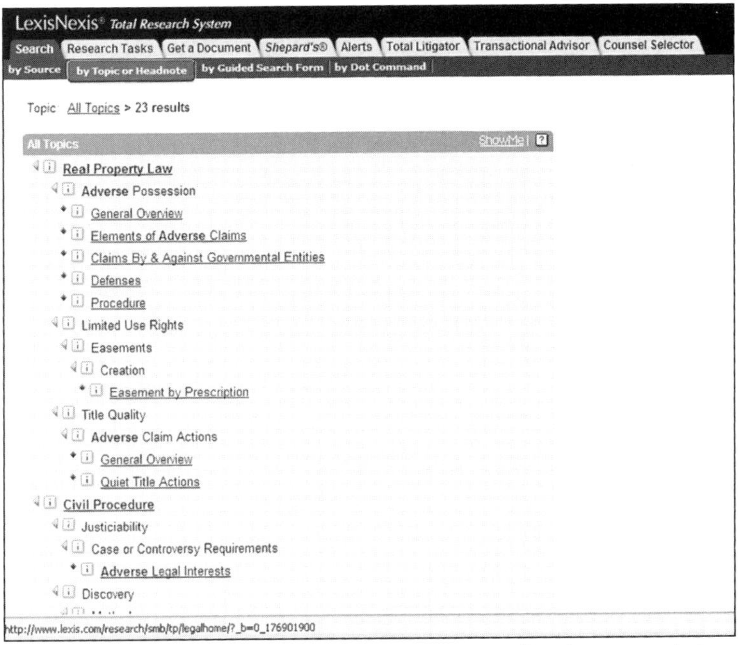

Source: LexisNexis, a division of Reed Elsevier Inc. All rights reserved. LexisNexis and the Knowledge Burst logo are registered trademarks of Reed Elsevier Properties Inc. and are used with the permission of LexisNexis.

sions of cases. Review these headnotes with the same care that you would review headnotes in a print digest. Skimming the entries is easier in online research because they are hyperlinked to the list of cases. To read relevant cases with the analytical attention needed for legal research, consider printing the cases.

B. Internet Subject Research

Most Internet sites do not have digest features. For example, both federal and state court sites generally do not yet allow searching by topic; instead, you must know the case name or docket number to access an opinion. However, topic-searching capability is likely to be-

Figure 3-13. KeySearch Search Page

Source: Westlaw. Reprinted with permission of West, a Thomson business.

come available in the near future, and the techniques above may be useful.

Even now, a subject search in a general search engine can produce useful results. A law firm may have posted links to recent judicial opinions or an attorney may have posted links to an outline of research on your very topic.

V. Reading and Analyzing Cases

After locating a possibly relevant case, you must read it, understand it, and analyze its potential relevance to the problem you are researching. This process is often challenging, time-consuming work. It is not unusual for a lawyer to spend hours reading (and re-reading) cases, especially in unfamiliar areas of law. This reading may be interrupted by references to a law dictionary to try to understand the terms used. The following strategies should make reading and analyzing cases more effective.

A. Reading Cases Effectively

Review the synopsis quickly to determine whether the case seems to be on point. If so, skim the headnotes to find the particular portion of the case that is relevant. Remember that one case may discuss several issues of law, only one or two of which may interest you. Go to the portion of the case identified by the relevant headnote and decide whether it is important for your project. If so, skim the entire case to get a feeling for what happened and why, focusing on the portion of the case identified by the relevant headnote.

After determining that a case is relevant, read the case slowly and carefully. Skip the parts that are obviously not pertinent to your problem. At the end of each paragraph or page, consider what you have read. If you cannot summarize it, try reading the material again.

Read the case again, this time taking notes. The notes may be in the form of a formal "case brief" or they may be scribbles that only you can understand. Regardless of the form, the process of taking notes will help you parse through, identify, and comprehend the essential concepts of the case. When preparing to write a legal document, the notes will assist you in organizing your analysis into an outline. Note that skimming text online or highlighting a printed page is often not sufficient to achieve thorough comprehension of judicial opinions.

B. Analyzing the Substance of Cases

If a case concerns the same legally significant facts as your client's situation and the court applies law on point for your problem, then the case is relevant and should be considered carefully as you analyze your problem. Legally significant facts are those that affect the court's decision. Some attorneys call these outcome-determinative facts or key facts. Which facts are legally significant depends on the case. The height of the defendant in a contract dispute is unlikely to be legally significant, but that fact may be critical in a criminal case where the only eyewitness testified that the thief was about five feet tall.

Rarely will research reveal a case with facts that are exactly the same as your client's situation. Rather, several cases may involve facts that are similar to your client's situation but not exactly the same. Your job is to determine whether the facts are similar enough for a court to apply the law in the same way and reach the same outcome. If the court reached a decision favorable to your client, you will highlight the similarities. If, on the other hand, the court reached an unfavorable decision from your client's perspective, you may argue that the case is distinguishable from yours based on its facts or that its reasoning is faulty. Note that you have an ethical duty to ensure that the court knows about a case directly on point, even if the outcome of that case is adverse to your client.

It is also unlikely that one case will address all aspects of your client's situation. Most legal claims have several elements or factors. *Elements* are required subparts of a claim, while *factors* are important aspects but all are not required for a claim to succeed. If a court decides that one element is not met, it might not discuss others. In a different case, the court may decide that two factors are so overwhelming that others have no impact on the outcome. In these circumstances, you would have to find other cases that analyze the other elements or factors.

After determining that a case is relevant to some portion of your analysis, you must decide how heavily it will weigh in your analysis. Two important points need to be considered here. One is the concept of *stare decisis*; the other is the difference between the holding of the case and dicta within that case.

Stare decisis means "to stand by things decided." This concept means that courts must follow prior opinions, ensuring consistency in the application of the law. *Stare decisis*, however, is limited to the courts within one jurisdiction. The Courts of Appeal of California must follow the decisions of the California Supreme Court, but not those of the courts of any other state. The concept of *stare decisis* also refers to a court with respect to its own opinions. A court of appeal, thus, should follow its own earlier cases in deciding new matters. If a court decides not to continue following its earlier cases, it is usually because of changes in society that have outdated the law of the earlier case, or because a new statute has been enacted that changes the legal landscape.

Under *stare decisis*, courts are required to follow the *holding* of prior cases. The holding is the court's ultimate decision on the matter of law at issue in the case. Other statements or observations included in the opinion are not binding; they are referred to as *dicta*. For example, in deciding whether passing a bad check through the window at a bank's drive-through facility was burglary, a court observed that a person putting his arm through a library chute to remove books would commit burglary. That observation was based on hypothetical facts and was not the basis of the court's decision. The observation is therefore dicta and is not binding on future courts, though it may be cited as persuasive authority.

After finding a number of relevant cases, you must synthesize them to state and explain the legal rule. Sometimes a court states the rule fully; if not, piece together the information from the relevant cases. Then use the analysis and facts of various cases to explain the law. Decide how the rule applies to the client's facts, and determine your conclusion. Note that this method of synthesis is much more than mere summaries of all the various cases. Legal analysis texts in the bibliography of this book explain synthesis in detail.

Chapter 4

Constitutions

California has had two constitutions. The first constitution was framed at a constitutional convention in September and October 1849 and ratified at an election on November 13, 1849, nearly a year before California became a state. A second constitutional convention met in 1879, and the voters ratified the new constitution on May 7, 1879. It became effective January 1, 1880, but is always referred to as the Constitution of 1879.

The provisions of the current California Constitution parallel many of the provisions of the United States Constitution, although the California Constitution provides for greater rights in some areas. Article I, section 1 lists the inalienable rights of California's citizens. Among those rights are "enjoying and defending life and liberty, acquiring, possessing, and protecting property, and pursuing and obtaining safety, happiness, and privacy."[1]

California has one of the longest constitutions in the United States because it covers many issues often thought of as being statutory in nature. (See Table 4-1.) For example, Article I, section 2 provides the news media with a shield against an adjudication of contempt by a judicial, legislative, or administrative body for refusing to disclose unpublished information or sources. Because of the breadth of issues covered by the California Constitution, it is wise to consider whether a constitutional provision affects a particular research problem.

---

1. Cal. Const. art. I, § 1.

Table 4-1. Articles of the Constitution of California

Article I	Declaration of Rights
Article II	Voting, Initiative and Referendum, and Recall
Article III	State of California
Article IV	Legislative
Article V	Executive
Article VI	Judicial
Article VII	Public Officers and Employees
Article IX	Education
Article X	Water
Article XA	Water Resources Development
Article XB	Marine Resources Protection Act of 1990
Article XI	Local Government
Article XII	Public Utilities
Article XIII	Taxation
Article XIIIA	[Tax Limitation]
Article XIIIB	Government Spending Limitation
Article XIIIC	[Voter Approval for Local Tax Levies]
Article XIIID	[Assessment and Property Related Fee Reform]
Article XIV	Labor Relations
Article XV	Usury
Article XVI	Public Finance
Article XVIII	Amending and Revising the Constitution
Article XIX	Motor Vehicle Revenues
Article XIXA	Loans from the Public Transportation Account or Local Transportation Funds
Article XIXB	Motor Vehicle Fuel Sales Tax Revenues and Transportation Improvement Funding
Article XX	Miscellaneous Subjects
Article XXI	Reapportionment of Senate, Assembly, Congressional and Board of Equalization Districts
Article XXII	[Architectural and Engineering Services]
Article XXXIV	Public Housing Project Law
Article XXXV	Medical Research

Note: Repealed and rejected articles are not listed.

I. Researching the California Constitution

The California Constitution is contained in both of the published statutory codes of California, *West's Annotated California Codes* and *Deering's California Codes Annotated*. The constitution appears in the first several volumes of both annotated codes. The index to the constitution appears in both code versions in the volume that contains the last section of the constitution. Between the final article of the constitution and the index, the publishers have included additional resources, including the text of the Constitution of 1849, the U.S. Constitution, and various federal statutes affecting California, including the act for admission of the state. These additional resources are not identical in both sources, so if possible check both code versions when looking for a specific document.

As explained in Chapters 1 and 2, begin research by generating a list of research terms from the facts and issues of your problem. Search the index for each term and record the references given. For example, searching the index in *West's Annotated California Codes* using the term "Searches and Seizures" leads to references to Article I, sections 13 and 24 of the California Constitution.

To find cases and other authorities that have discussed a certain provision of the state constitution, look for the editorial material that follows the text of the particular section of each relevant article. This material includes historical notes, cross-references to statutes, citations to relevant law review articles, references to other materials published by the same publisher, references to analogous sections of the United States Constitution, and case annotations. These annotations are called "Notes of Decisions," and they reference cases and attorney general opinions. Each annotation contains a brief summary of the source referenced and its citation, which will enable you to locate the actual source. (See Table 4-2.) Be sure not to rely on the short summary; reading the text of the source itself is the only way to analyze its relevance to your research.

The Notes of Decisions are divided into subject-matter categories chosen by the publisher. In *West's Annotated California Codes,* these categories are outlined at the beginning of the Notes of Decisions;

Figure 4-2. Excerpt of Annotations for California Constitution

Art. I, Section 13	◄─────── Caption for Article 1, section 13
I. IN GENERAL 1–40	
II. ISSUANCE OF WARRANT 41–130	
III. SEARCHES AND SEIZURES 131–450	◄─────── Outline for anno-
IV. ADMISSIBILITY OF EVIDENCE 451–510	tations relevant to
V. PRACTICE AND PROCEDURE 511–570	this constitutional
NOTES OF DECISIONS	provision

135. Knock and announce, searches and seizures

Under both the Fourth Amendment and the state ◄─── Annotation to
constitution's search and seizure provision, a person   a case from
may challenge the legality of a search or seizure only if   the California
he can show a personal interest in the privacy of the   Court of Appeal
place searched or the item seized; he may not vicari-
ously challenge the alleged violation of another's interests. People v. Hoag (App. 3 Dist. 2000) 100
Cal.Rptr.2d 556, 83 Cal.App.4th 1198, review denied.

Source: *West's Annotated California Codes*, volume 1A, page 174 (2002). Reprinted with permission of West, a Thomson business.

there is no similar outline in *Deering's California Codes Annotated*. If the version you are using has an outline, begin research in the annotations by looking over the outline for the area that is most pertinent to your research. This initial scanning of the outline is particularly important for sections that have been discussed in many cases and attorney general opinions, such as in the example in Table 4-2. Note that the annotations listed in these sources do not represent every authority that may be relevant to your research. To find additional cases on point, use the strategies discussed in Chapter 3. Chapter 9 explains using secondary sources as research tools.

The California Constitution is also available electronically. The text of the constitution may be found on two fee-based services, LexisNexis and Westlaw. These services contain the same annotations that appear in *Deering's California Codes Annotated* and *West's Annotated California Codes*, respectively. Research techniques using these two services are discussed more fully in Chapter 2. The full text is also available for free on the state's website at www.leginfo.ca.gov/const.html.[2] The website contains a link to the Table of Contents as well as a search engine that allows searching by keyword.

II. Interpreting the California Constitution

California courts interpret a constitutional provision by considering the intent of those who enacted it. "To determine that intent, courts look first to the language of the constitutional text, giving the words their ordinary meaning."[3] In determining the "ordinary meaning" of the words, California courts may look to dictionaries, including legal dictionaries, and to decisions of other courts considering the same or similar language.[4] However, the words of the constitutional provision "must receive a liberal, practical common sense construction."[5] Moreover, the "literal language of enactments may be disregarded to avoid absurd results and to fulfill the apparent intent of the framers."[6]

When the language of the provision is not clear, California courts look to the source of the constitutional provision in interpreting its meaning. For provisions of the Constitution of 1879 that are still in effect, the court can look to the proceedings of the constitutional convention of 1879, as well as to the daily journal of the debates. Both are difficult to find in most libraries, although microfiche copies are available through the Congressional Information Services (CIS) *State Constitutional Conventions* set, which some libraries have.

---

2. The text of the Constitution of 1849 is available on the website for the State Archives at www.ss.ca.gov/archives/level3_const1849txt.html.

3. *Leone v. Med. Bd. of Cal.*, 22 Cal. 4th 660, 665, 94 Cal. Rptr. 2d 61, 64, 995 P.2d 191, 194 (2000).

4. *Id.* at 666, 94 Cal. Rptr. 2d at 64, 995 P.2d at 194–195.

5. *L.A. Metro. Transit Auth. v. Pub. Util. Commn.*, 59 Cal. 2d 863, 869, 31 Cal. Rptr. 463, 466, 382 P.2d 583, 586 (1963).

6. *Amador Valley Jt. Union High Sch. Dist. v. St. Bd. of Equalization*, 22 Cal. 3d 208, 245, 149 Cal. Rptr. 239, 258, 583 P.2d 1281, 1300 (1978).

Because the current California Constitution has been amended repeatedly, your research is likely to involve a section that was not part of the Constitution of 1879. The constitution may be *revised* through a constitutional convention called by the legislature.[7] It may be *amended* through either a proposal passed by a two-thirds vote of each house of the legislature[8] or by a voter initiative;[9] in either case, voters then have the opportunity to approve or reject the proposal or initiative.[10] The distinction between revision and amendment relates to the scope of the proposed change, and it can be crucial to the viability of the attempted change. The California Supreme Court has held that revision, which is a more sweeping change to the constitution than amendment, must be done through a constitutional convention and may not be accomplished through the initiative process.[11] Therefore, if you are researching a proposed change to the state constitution, you should first determine its scope.

The initiative process was adopted in a number of states during the Progressive Era in the early 20th century in response to legislative corruption. California adopted it in 1911, largely to address the control of the legislature by the railroad companies. This process allows voters to propose amendments to the state constitution by placing measures on the election ballot. Voters begin the process by submitting a petition with at least a certain number of signatures of qualified voters; this number is equal to 8% of the number of voters in the previous gubernatorial election (it is 5% for an initiative that proposes a statute).[12]

---

7. Cal. Const. art. XVIII, § 2. California has not had a constitutional convention since 1879.

8. Cal. Const. art. XVIII, § 1.

9. Cal. Const. art. XVIII, § 3.

10. Cal. Const. art. XVIII, § 4.

11. *McFadden v. Jordan*, 32 Cal. 2d 330, 332–333, 196 P.2d 787, 789 (1948).

12. Cal. Const. art. II, § 8(b). The lower percentage for statutes was approved by the voters in 1966 as an effort to encourage statutes rather than constitutional amendments. Joseph R. Grodin, Calvin R. Massey & Richard B. Cunningham, *The California State Constitution: A Reference Guide* 69–70 (Greenwood Press 1993).

Because the initiative process has become increasingly popular since the success of the property tax initiative Proposition 13 in 1976, the ballot may contain more than one initiative that addresses the same subject. If the voters pass two or more conflicting initiatives, the constitution includes the unusual rule that the measure that received the highest number of votes in the election prevails.[13]

If a court must look behind the wording of a section of the constitution added or amended by voter initiative, it looks for evidence of the voters' intent in the ballot summary and the arguments and analysis presented in the California *Voter Information Guide.* That pamphlet is prepared by the Office of Legislative Counsel before each election and distributed to all registered voters by the secretary of state. Complete sets of these pamphlets from 1911 forward may be found in a few larger libraries, but most law libraries are likely to have voter pamphlets from only the last decade or two. The California Secretary of State's Office maintains an electronic database of voter pamphlets dating back to March 1996 at www.ss.ca.gov/elections/elections_i.htm. From that site, you can access a searchable database of California ballot measures dating back to 1911, maintained by the University of California Hastings College of Law, by clicking on a link to "California Ballot Propositions Database." The Hastings site contains a word search to find specific voter pamphlets.

III. United States Constitution

The federal constitution is the foundational law of the United States. As noted above, it is published along with the California Constitution in both *Deering's California Codes Annotated* and *West's Annotated California Codes.* It is also available in print in the first several volumes of *United States Code Annotated* and *United States Code Service.* These series are explained in Chapter 5.

The United States Constitution is also available online at both state and federal websites. Some addresses of relevant sites include:

---

13. Cal. Const. art. II, § 10.

- www.loc.gov/law/guide, a site maintained by the Law Library of Congress with links to a wide range of sites that include the text of the U.S. Constitution, as well as commentaries and annotations, some of which also provide search engines;
- www.law.emory.edu/index.php?id=3080, a university site that provides a search engine; and
- www.findlaw.com/casecode/constitution, a free research site with a search engine.

Chapter 5

Statutes

In the hierarchy of legal authority in the United States, statutes come just below constitutions and ahead of regulations and cases as controlling sources of law. Therefore, for almost any research problem, you should first check to see if there is a statute that affects your client's rights or responsibilities. Statutes create new rights or responsibilities when the legislature decides that the law needs to address a new issue, such as anti-discrimination laws or seat belt laws. The legislature has also taken many common law rights and duties and enacted them into statutory law. For example, criminal law has been made almost completely statutory, sometimes by enacting the common law elements, sometimes by changing the elements, and sometimes by creating new crimes, such as stalking.[1] Even if your client's problem is not governed by a statute, you may still need to consult the relevant code to find the statute of limitations that governs how long you have to bring a claim.

I. Researching California Statutes in Print

Despite the availability of online sources for California statutes, many attorneys find that research is initially more effective using print codes. This chapter begins with print sources, then covers online sources for statutory research.

---

1. Section 646.9 of the California Penal Code defines and criminalizes stalking. It was added to the Penal Code in 1990.

Table 5-1. Outline for Statutory Research in Print

---

1. Look up research terms in the index of the appropriate statutory compilation to find references to relevant statutes.
2. Locate, read, and analyze the statutes in the main volumes. If there is a pocket part or paper supplement, check for recent changes in the language of the statute.
3. Refer to annotations following the statutory language to find citations to cases and other authorities that interpret, apply, or analyze the statute.
4. If the resource you are using has a pocket part or supplementary volume, check that for more recent annotations.
5. Read and analyze the relevant cases.

A. California Codes

California has two print statutory compilations: *Deering's California Codes Annotated*, published by LexisNexis, and *West's Annotated California Codes*, published by West. The language of the statutes should be identical in both sets, so either version can be used for your research. The research steps are the same in both versions, as outlined in Table 5-1.

California statutes can be enacted by either the legislature or by the voters through the referendum and initiative process, which is similar to the initiative process for constitutional amendments, discussed in Chapter 4. Enacted statutes are then *codified*, meaning that they are grouped according to subject matter.[2] As each new statute is enacted, it is placed within the appropriate subject-matter code.

California statutes are grouped into 29 individual subject-matter codes, which are listed in Table 5-2. Each of these codes is then di-

---

2. A few statutes and some initiative acts are never codified.

Table 5-2. California Statutory Codes

Business and Professions	Insurance
Civil	Labor
Civil Procedure	Military and Veterans
Commercial	Penal
Corporations	Probate
Education	Public Contract
Elections	Public Resources
Evidence	Public Utilities
Family	Revenue and Taxation
Financial	Streets and Highways
Fish and Game	Unemployment Insurance
Food and Agriculture	Vehicle
Government	Water
Harbors and Navigation	Welfare and Institutions
Health and Safety	

vided into sections. For example, California Penal Code §451 states what constitutes arson. The citation to this statute is Cal. Penal Code §451. Note that California lawyers refer to Cal. Penal Code §451 as both a "statute" and a "code section."

Within various codes, sections may be grouped according to subtopics, though all the codes do not use the same divisions. To continue the arson example, in the Penal Code, Title 13 addresses crimes against property, Chapter 1 concerns the crime of arson, and Section 451 states what constitutes arson.[3] Subdivisions of a section are indicated by (a), (b), (c), etc. Subdivision (a) of §451 provides punishment of up to nine years in prison for arson that causes great bodily injury. The citation to this subdivision is Cal. Penal Code §451(a). Be careful because older statutes may include a letter without parentheses, such as §403a, which should not be confused with subdivision (a) of a different §403, which is printed as §403(a).

---

3. California lawyers informally use the term "statute" to refer both to the section and to the chapter.

B. The Research Process in Print Codes

How you begin the process of researching in California statutes depends on what information you have before you start. If you know which statute controls your situation, you can go directly to the volumes on the shelf. The name of each code is printed on the spine of the volume or volumes that contain that code. For example, "Health and Safety" and "Penal" are listed on the spines of the books, and the codes are shelved in alphabetical order. Simply find the appropriate code and then look at the section numbers listed on the spine of each volume for that code. Page through the relevant volume to find the statute's section number.

More often, you will begin research knowing only the client's facts. In that situation, follow the outline given in Table 5-1 at the beginning of this chapter, which is explained below.

1. Search the Index for Research Terms

To find all the statutes that may relate to your issue, develop an expansive list of research terms. Take these research terms to the General Index volumes shelved at the end of either *Deering's California Codes Annotated* or *West's Annotated California Codes*. Search for every one of your research terms. As you find the terms in the index volumes, write down all the statutory references given.

Do not stop reviewing the Index after finding just one or two statute references; several statutes may address your issue. Note that "et seq." refers to the section listed and the sections that follow it. Sometimes a research term will be included in the index but will be followed by a cross-reference to another index term. Referring to that term may lead you to other relevant statutes. See Figure 5-3 for an example of an index section.

Figure 5-3. Selected Entries for ARSON in *Deering's* Index

ARSON, Pen §§ 450 to 457.1
Attempts, Pen § 455
Forests fires, PubRes § 4418
Inhabited structures or property, Pen §§ 451, 452
Pecuniary motives, Pen § 456
Solicitation, Pen § 653f

Source: *Deering's California Codes Annotated, Index*, page 126 (2007). Reproduced with permission of LexisNexis Matthew Bender. Further reproduction of any kind is strictly prohibited.

2. Find and Read the Statutory Language

Both *Deering's* and *West's* contain the text of each statute, arranged in numerical order. For each statutory citation you found in the General Index, select the volume that contains the code name and section number in the citation, and then find the statute itself. Because the print volumes are not republished every year, the publishers include a pocket part or paperbound supplement that includes new statutes enacted since the bound volume was published, as well as additions to and deletions from statutes in the bound volume. Check the pocket part to see if the language of the statute has changed since the hardbound volume was published. Both *Deering's* and *West's* reprint the entire statutory section in the pocket part if the statute has been amended. *Deering's* indicates additions and changes by using italics and indicates deletions by inserting asterisks, while *West's* indicates additions and changes by underlining and indicates deletions by inserting asterisks. If the hardbound volume is particularly old, the pocket part may be too large to fit in the pocket and will be replaced by a separate softbound volume, which should be shelved next to the hardbound volume. Failing to check the pocket part or softbound volume can be a serious error, so be sure to do it before you do anything else.

This next step is the most important: *Read* the statute very carefully, in both the main volume and the pocket part. Too many researchers fail to take the time necessary to read the language of the

Figure 5-4. Example California Code Section

---

§ 451. Arson of structure, forest land or property; great bodily injury; inhabited structure or property; owned property; punishment.

A person is guilty of arson when he or she willfully and maliciously sets fire to or burns or causes to be burned or who aids, counsels, or procures the burning of, any structure, forest land, or property.

    (a) Arson that causes great bodily injury is a felony punishable by imprisonment in the state prison for five, seven, or nine years.

    (b) Arson that causes an inhabited structure or inhabited property to burn is a felony punishable by imprisonment in the state prison for three, five, or eight years.

    (c) Arson of a structure or forest land is a felony punishable by imprisonment in the state prison for two, four, or six years.

Source: *West's Annotated California Codes*, Penal Code Sections 319 to 593g, page 298 (1999). Reprinted with permission of West, a Thomson business.

statute and consider all its implications before deciding whether it is relevant to the research problem. And because statutes are the product of legislative compromises and negotiations, their language is often not clear enough to convey all possible meanings on one reading. Therefore, careful research may require multiple readings of the statutory language before you can fully understand its meaning and legal relevance.

In addition, you may need to read more than one code section and even other, related code sections. One section may contain general provisions, while others contain definitions and exceptions.

The example code section in Figure 5-4 provides a definition of the crime of arson and indicates the possible punishments, depending on what kind of property was burned and whether anyone was injured. However, in order to know if your client acted "maliciously," you would have to look at Section 450 of the Penal Code, which defines the term.

To guarantee that you understand the statute, break it into its elements. Using bullet points or an outline format is helpful for identifying the individual elements. Connecting words and punctuation

Table 5-5. Elements of Arson

- a person is guilty of arson who
  - willfully <u>and</u> maliciously
- acts by
  - setting fire to
  - burning
  - causing to be burned, <u>or</u>
  - aiding, counseling, or procuring the burning of
- any
  - structure,
  - forest land, <u>or</u>
  - property

may help delineate the relationships between the various elements. For example, "and" means that all the elements must be present for the statute to apply, while "or" means that only one of the elements connected by "or" needs to be present. Table 5-5 breaks the first part of California Penal Code § 451 into its elements. Note that the bold words following the section number in Figure 5-4 are not part of the statutory language and should be not included in your outline. These words have been supplied by the publisher, and they are not identical in *Deering's* and *West's*.

3. Find Cases that Interpret or Apply the Statute

Legislatures write statutes to apply to a wide variety of factual situations, so they are intentionally broad and often vague or ambiguous. Unless the relevant statute is very recent, it likely has been interpreted by courts. The resulting judicial opinions will help you determine if and how the statute applies to your client's specific facts.

Both *Deering's* and *West's* annotated codes contain annotations to cases that have interpreted each code section that has been part of a court case. In *West's*, the annotations are the same case annotations used in West digests and the headnotes of cases in West reporters (discussed in Chapter 3). The annotations in *Deering's* are written by its publisher, LexisNexis, so their wording differs from the wording in the annotations written by West. However, the concept is the same in both instances.

These annotations are divided topically. For instance, in addition to looking at the subdivision of the arson statute that defines "maliciously," you can also find annotations that interpret that term. You can also find cases that interpret terms not defined in the statute, such as "burning." If the hardbound volume has a pocket part or supplement, it may contain annotations to cases, which will be more recent than those in the hardbound volume.

The editorial material in both code sets includes other research aids such as cross-references to other statutes that relate to the arson statute, law review and other journal articles about the substance or application of the statute, and references to other publications produced by the publisher. Since the two annotated codes have different publishers, they may refer to different law review and journal articles, and the references to other publications are different in each set. However, regardless of the annotated code you use, the case notes and the references to other statutes and publications provide an extremely helpful starting point for researching any problem involving this particular statute.

C. Other Helpful Features of Print Annotated Codes

In both *Deering's* and *West's*, immediately following the text of the statute you will find in parentheses the enactment and amendment history of the section. This history shows when the statute was first enacted, and the years, session law numbers, and effective date for each amendment in chronological order. Thus, the most recent amendment will be listed last. Under this parenthetical, the publisher also includes notes detailing the changes made by each amendment. These histories are extremely useful because a statute can be enforced only if it was in effect at the time of the event on which the criminal charge or civil suit is based. You should read these sections carefully to make sure that the statute actually applies to your client's situation.

II. Researching California Statutes Online

Researching California statutes online can be one of the most difficult forms of online research unless you have the citation to the appropriate statute. You can retrieve a statute by using the "Get a Document" feature on LexisNexis or the "Find by citation" feature on Westlaw. You will not need to check for a pocket part or supplement, of course, because online services are updated almost immediately when statutory language changes. Once you have the relevant statutory section, both systems allow you to move to adjacent sections so that you can see the entire statute. On LexisNexis, click on "Book Browse" and then click on the arrows alongside the statutory code name and section number. On Westlaw, there is no need to move into a different format; just click on "Previous Section" or "Next Section" alongside the code name and section number on the screen in which the statute first appears.

If you do not have a citation to the statute, online statutory research is more difficult. The California Codes are long, and many statutes may share the same language. In addition, any time that an annotation quotes the language of a statute, an online search will pick up that language. Finally, as noted above, statutes are often written using very general language, which means that the same general language may turn up in statutes having very different subject matters. Nevertheless, if you need to do statutory research online, either because you prefer online research or because print sources are unavailable, follow the steps outlined in Table 5-6.

In addition to LexisNexis and Westlaw, you can also find California statutes in several free online sources. However, these sites will give you the statutory language only; to get the references to cases that have interpreted and applied the statute or to secondary sources that have discussed the statute, you must use one of the fee-based systems.

Table 5-6. Outline for Statutory Research Online

1. Choose the appropriate online library or database.
2. Construct either a terms-and-connectors search or a natural-language search of the full text of the statutory codes.
3. Alternatively, skim the Table of Contents for a relevant code name and expand the list by clicking the "plus" symbol.
4. As another alternative, review an online Index to the California statutes, and conduct a search for your terms.

The State of California provides a searchable database for statutes at www.leginfo.ca.gov/calaw.html. To find the relevant statute, however, you must know the name of the code you want to search; for example, to find the arson statute, you must choose the Penal Code before you enter the search term "arson." You can access this site directly or through various law library sites, such as that of the Law Library of Congress at www.loc.gov/law/guide, which provides access to the statutes of all states and of the federal government. As with other free systems, these databases include only the text of the statutes with no case references or other editorial aids.

III. Applying and Interpreting California Statutes

In general, applying a statute means (1) reading its words carefully, (2) understanding its elements, (3) reading any related or referenced statutes, (4) analyzing cases that apply or interpret the statutes, and (5) applying the law to the facts of your client's case. In the fourth step, you will sometimes need to consider *how* the California courts interpret statutory language.

Fundamentally, California courts seek to "ascertain and effectuate legislative intent."[4] "An equally basic rule of statutory construction is,

---

4. *Kimmel v. Goland*, 51 Cal. 3d 202, 208, 793 P.2d 524, 527, 271 Cal. Rptr. 191, 194 (1990).

however, that courts are bound to give effect to statutes according to the usual, ordinary import of the language employed in framing them."[5] In other words, courts should apply the plain meaning of the words. The court should, where possible, look at every word and phrase, and should avoid a construction that makes language superfluous.[6] In addition, the words should be construed in context with the statutory purpose and the entire statutory framework in mind.[7] Finally, the statute should be interpreted, if possible, in harmony with any applicable constitutional provisions.[8] If the words of the statute are clear and unambiguous, the court should not look to any extrinsic aids to determine the legislature's intent. However, if more than one construction of the language is reasonable, the court may look to legislative history to ascertain legislative intent.[9]

Thus, you should look at the words of the statute to see if they are clear and unambiguous. If they are, you should apply their plain meaning to your analysis of how the statute applies. If they are ambiguous in the sense of there being more than one reasonable interpretation, turn to legislative history, discussed in Chapter 6.

As you begin to understand the statute and develop your analysis, follow these guidelines in drafting your document:

- Quote the relevant portion of the statute in enough detail to provide context without overwhelming your reader with unnecessary language.
- Omit parts of the statute that do not apply to your facts.
- Paraphrase parts of the statute that are difficult for your reader to understand and are not critical to your analysis. If quoting

---

5. *Cal. Teachers Assn. v. San Diego Community College Dist.*, 28 Cal. 3d 692, 698, 621 P.2d 856, 858–859, 170 Cal. Rptr. 817, 820 (1981).

6. *Moyer v. Workmen's Compen. Apps. Bd.*, 10 Cal. 3d 222, 230, 514 P.2d 1224, 1229, 110 Cal. Rptr. 144, 149 (1973).

7. *Id.*

8. *In re Marquez*, 30 Cal. 4th 14, 20, 65 P.3d 403, 406, 131 Cal. Rptr. 2d 911, 914 (2003).

9. *People v. Robles*, 23 Cal. 4th 1106, 1111, 5 P.3d 176, 180, 99 Cal. Rptr. 2d 120, 123 (2000).

requires you to use many ellipses to indicate omitted language, it may be better to paraphrase. But be careful not to change the meaning of the statutory language.

IV. Researching the Statutes of Other States

Every state has codified statutes, but the names vary from state to state. Examples include *Hawaii Revised Statutes, Pennsylvania Consolidated Statutes,* and *South Dakota Codified Laws.* A national citation manual will list the name of the statutory code for each state.

While the same basic process applies to statutory research in other states, there may be some important differences. California is unusual in having both a subject name and a section number; only New York and Texas follow this pattern. Most states number their statutes using a combination of numerals and decimal points, although not all states use the same numbering system. For example, the following citations all indicate a statutory section of definitions relating to arson: Ariz. Rev. Stat. Ann. §13-1701 (Arizona); Nev. Rev. Stat. §205.005 (Nevada); Or. Rev. Stat. §164.305 (Oregon); and Wash. Rev. Code §9A.48.010 (Washington).

V. Researching Federal Statutes

The official text of federal statutes is published in *United States Code* (U.S.C.). Similar to the organization of California statutes, federal statutes are codified under subject-matter titles, each of which is numbered. There are fifty-one titles in U.S.C., and each title is further subdivided into section numbers. To cite a federal statute, you must include the number of the title and the number of the specific section. For example, the statute under which the Environmental Protection Agency regulates emission standards for new cars is 42 U.S.C. §7521 (2006). Title 42 is devoted to Public Health and Welfare, and 7521 is the specific section in the Clean Air Act that is assigned to new car emission standards. That volume of U.S.C. was published in 2006.

U.S.C. is updated infrequently and does not include any annotations or other editorial research aids, so it has very limited research value. The absence of annotations and other editorial aids also limits the usefulness of the online sites maintained by the federal government, such as GPO Access, at www.gpoaccess.gov. The sources you are more likely to use are *United States Code Annotated* (U.S.C.A.) and *United States Code Service* (U.S.C.S.), published by West and Lexis Publishing respectively. These annotated codes can also be found online through Westlaw and LexisNexis. If the current text of the statute is not available in U.S.C., however, citing U.S.C.A. or U.S.C.S. in print is preferred over citing an online code.

Both U.S.C.A. and U.S.C.S. contain the text of federal statutes and references to related research sources. Both publications include annotations that refer to cases interpreting or applying the statute. Some researchers feel that U.S.C.A. provides more case annotations than U.S.C.S., while U.S.C.S. provides more helpful tables and better information on court rules. For the beginning researcher, both are probably of equal value, and checking both will provide more case annotations than will using either one by itself. In practice, only one series is likely to be available in a private library, so use whichever one you have access to.

In print, U.S.C.A. and U.S.C.S. are updated through pocket parts and softbound supplements, similar to the pocket parts and softbound supplements for the California statutory compilations. When only portions of the statute have changed, the pocket part may refer to the unchanged language in the hardbound volume. Other pocket parts are cumulative, so a modified statute will be reprinted in full.

Both annotated federal codes contain information other than statutes and research annotations. For example, they provide references to federal regulations and executive orders. Both U.S.C.S. and U.S.C.A. include helpful tables, such as tables listing statutes by their popular names. These tables appear at the end of each series in softbound volumes, along with the General Index for each series, which is also softbound. Finally, as explained in the next part, both contain federal court rules.

VI. Researching Court Rules

Court rules are frequently published in statutory codifications, and both of California's annotated codes do so. Court rules govern litigation practice from the filing of initial pleadings through the final appeal. Rules dictate litigation details ranging from the correct caption for pleadings to the rules of procedure for the probate courts and rules on both civil and criminal appeals. Ethical rules may also govern who can practice law in the state, including rules about disciplinary proceedings and legal education.[10]

Court rules are primary authority, even though the court or legislature responsible for them has delegated rule-making power to a council, committee, or other body. Success in litigation may depend as much on compliance with these rules as on the merits of the claim.

A. California Court Rules

The Judicial Council of California is the policy-making body for courts of California.[11] It has adopted California's Rules of Court, which apply to all courts in the state. Both *Deering's California Codes Annotated* and *West's Annotated California Codes* publish multiple volumes of California court rules. In *Deering's*, they appear under the title "Rules of Court," while in *West's* they are under "Court Rules." However, the rules included are the same. In addition, both publishers include State Bar Rules in the last volume of the court rules. These rules relate to the California State Bar, its members, programs, and relationships with other entities. As with California statutes, the Rules of Court and the State Bar Rules are available electronically on LexisNexis and Westlaw.

The California Rules of Court were divided into ten titles following a reorganization adopted by the Judicial Council in 2006 (see

---

10. Title 9, Chapter 2 of the California Rules of Court covers Attorney Disciplinary Proceedings, and Chapter 3 covers Legal Education.

11. *See* www.courtinfo.ca.gov/jc.

Table 5-7. California Rules of Court

Title 1	Rules Applicable to all Courts
Title 2	Trial Court Rules
Title 3	Civil Rules
Title 4	Criminal Rules
Title 5	Family and Juvenile Rules
Title 6	[Reserved]
Title 7	Probate Rules
Title 8	Appellate Rules
Title 9	Rules on Law Practice, Attorneys, and Judges
Title 10	Judicial Administration Rules

Table 5-7). The reorganization repealed former rules, added new rules, and renumbered existing rules. Because of this reorganization, you will need to use a Derivation Table created by the Judicial Council to translate the old rule numbers into the new rule numbers. For example, the rule governing sanctions for violation of the court rules for civil proceedings, formerly Rule 227, is now Rule 2.30 in the reorganized Rules of Court. This derivation table is printed in both *Deering's* and *West's* in the beginning of the first volume of court rules.

The numbering system for the reorganized rules consists of two numbers separated by a decimal point. The first number, a number between one and ten, reflects the title. The number following the decimal point is a one-, two-, three-, or four-digit number, and these numbers rise progressively through the title. For example, the first rule in Title 2 is numbered 2.1, and the next rule is 2.2, but the fourth rule is 2.20, and the seventh rule is 2.100. Thus, to find a particular rule when you know its number, look in the correct title as indicated by the first number, and then look to the numbers after the decimal point, paying close attention to how many numbers there are. For example, in Title 3 you will find Rule 3.1, Rule 3.10, Rule 3.100, and Rule 3.1000. Each of them is a different rule, and only Rules 3.1 and 3.10 are in the same subdivision of Title 3.

The California Rules of Court and local rules enacted by each Superior Court are also available online at www.courtinfo.ca.gov/rules.

Although both *Deering's* and *West's* update their print volumes with pocket parts, because the rules change frequently, this site is the best source for the rules. Click on the "Local Rules" link to reach a menu of rules for each Superior Court, organized by county. When practicing in any Superior Court in California, therefore, you must check both the California Rules of Court and the local rules to be sure your filings are technically correct.

Rules are written in outline form like statutes, and they should be read like statutes. Read each word carefully, refer to cross-referenced rules, and scan other rules nearby to see whether they are related.

As with the other volumes in the series, the publishers in both *Deering's* and *West's* have included annotations to cases that have applied the rule or its predecessor rule. *West's* includes an "Advisory Committee Comment" when one is available following the text of the rule, while *Deering's* puts these comments in footnotes. The comments are similar to legislative history for the rule and are persuasive authority only.[12]

Finally, both *Deering's* and *West's* publish softbound volumes of California Judicial Council forms. These forms are for use in the courts, and they cover a vast array of pleadings and other court forms. The forms are also available online at www.courtinfo.ca.gov/forms in PDF format.

B. Federal Court Rules

Similar rules exist on the federal level. They are published in U.S.C., U.S.C.A., U.S.C.S., and by the individual federal courts. Federal rules are available on LexisNexis, Westlaw, and various court websites.

---

12. Advisory committees advise the Judicial Council "in studying the condition of court business, improving judicial administration, and performing other council responsibilities." Members of advisory committees are appointed by the Chief Justice of the Supreme Court as chair of the Judicial Council from judges, court officials, lawyers, and members of the public. *See* www.courtinfo.ca.gov/jc/advisorycommittees.htm.

Placement of the rules varies among the print statutory publications. In U.S.C. and U.S.C.A., for example, the Federal Rules of Appellate Procedure appear just after Title 28, whose topic is "Judiciary and Judicial Procedure." In U.S.C.S., those rules are found at the end of all titles in separate volumes devoted to rules. As at the state level, each court may also have its own rules that either replace or supplement the general federal court rules. Thus, for example, the rules of the Eastern District of California may vary considerably from the rules of the neighboring Northern District of California. The easiest way to find these local rules is on the website of the U.S. courts, at www.uscourts.gov/rules.

Cases relevant to federal rules can be located using the annotated codes, or by referring to *Federal Practice Digest*, *Federal Rules Service* (rules of procedure), and *Federal Rules of Evidence Service*. Treatises on federal rules are covered in Chapter 9, Part IV.A.

Chapter 6

Legislative History

This chapter covers the process by which the California Legislature enacts laws. It begins with an overview of the legislative process and then describes *bill tracking*, the monitoring of current bills that may or may not ultimately become law.

Next, the chapter explains how to research the *legislative history* of a statute that has already been enacted. Legislative history research is most often relevant in litigation when a lawyer needs to convince the court to interpret a statute in a way that is favorable to the client's position.[1] Understanding the legislative process is often important in making a legislative intent argument because finding the legislature's intent in passing a statute may require the following types of analysis: (a) comparing various iterations of the bill that was eventually enacted into law, (b) reading statements by key legislators during the legislative debate over the bill, or (c) considering the understanding of the measure conveyed to legislators prior to key votes in the form of bill analyses by the legislature's professional committee staff.

I. The Legislative Process

The California Legislature contains two houses, the Senate and the Assembly.[2] The California Senate has forty members who serve four-

---

1. In fact, the California Code of Civil Procedure requires that when a court construes a statute, it must determine the intent of the legislature if possible. Cal. Civ. Proc. Code Ann. § 1859 (West 2007).

2. *See* Cal. Const. art. IV, § 1.

year terms, and the Assembly has eighty members who serve two-year terms. Terms are limited under the provisions of Proposition 140, an initiative approved by the voters in 1990. Senators can serve no more than two terms (eight years) and members of the Assembly can serve no more than three terms (six years).[3]

Each house has its own website. The Senate's is www.senate.ca.gov, and the Assembly's is www.assembly.ca.gov. Both contain information about legislators, pending legislation, committees, and other legislative matters. A separate site is maintained by the Office of Legislative Counsel, a nonpartisan public agency that serves as counsel to the legislature, to provide information on legislation.[4] That address is www.leginfo.ca.gov.

A legislative session in California lasts for two years. Each session begins on the first Monday in December of each even-numbered year. Sessions are numbered, however, with the odd year first and the even year second (e.g., 2007–2008).

The legislative process for enacting or amending laws in California is similar to that of other states and the federal legislature, the United States Congress. One specific requirement for all California statutes is that their titles must be read three times in each chamber of the legislature. Table 6-1 shows the progression of an idea from bill to statute and notes the documents generated at each step that are important in legal research. The next section of this chapter discusses the key sources in which legislative documents are published.

II. California Legislative Publications

Whether you want to track the progress of a current bill or research the history of an enacted statute, it helps to be familiar with the documents produced by the California Legislature during the legislative process. Some of these documents will be useful for bill track-

---

3. *See* Cal. Const. art IV, §§ 1.5 & 2.
4. The office and duties of the legislative counsel are statutorily defined. Cal. Govt. Code Ann. §§ 10200–10242.5 (West 2005).

Table 6-1. How a Bill Becomes a Law

Legislative Action	Documents Produced
An idea for legislation is suggested by a legislator, an agency, the governor, citizens, or lobbyists. A legislator who agrees to initiate the legislation sends the idea and proposed language to the Legislative Counsel for drafting. One or more legislators may sponsor the resulting bill.	The text of a **bill** is of paramount importance. If enacted, the bill's requirements or prohibitions may affect a client's interests. Even if a modified version is passed, comparing the original to the final version can help determine legislative intent.
The bill is introduced by a legislator in either the Senate or the Assembly. It is assigned a number, its title is read, and it is assigned to the appropriate standing committee. If the bill has a fiscal impact, it is also assigned to the Senate Appropriations Committee or the Assembly Ways and Means Committee for separate consideration. This is the first reading of the bill.	The bill is printed. The Legislative Counsel prepares a **digest** of the bill, which is printed on the first page of the bill. The **digest** summarizes the proposed changes in existing law, shows the number of votes needed to pass the bill, and indicates if the bill includes an appropriation of funds.
The committee schedules the bill for hearing. The hearing cannot occur until 30 days following the introduction and first reading, although this rule can be waived by a three-quarters vote of the house.	The **Daily File** has a schedule of committee meetings with dates that the bill is to be heard in committee. The staff of the committee prepares a **bill analysis**.
The committee holds a hearing. The bill's author presents the bill to the committee. Testimony may be taken in support or opposition.	Committee meetings are open to the public, but no record is required to be made and hearings of standing committees are almost never published. (They may be recorded and may be available in the archives of the California Channel.)
The committee votes on the bill, and the chair of the committee reports the committee recommendation to that house. The committee recommendation may be: Do pass; Do pass, as amended; or Be amended.	The committee vote is recorded and published in the *Journal* of that house. The committee's recommendation is reported in the *Journal* and the **Daily History**.
If the bill is passed by the committee, it is read a second time in the house of origin and placed "on file" for the third reading.	The **Daily File** lists bills scheduled for second reading. If the bill was reported out of committee with amendments and these amendments are adopted on the floor of that house, the bill is **reprinted**. The Legislative Counsel's **digest** is revised each time the bill is amended to reflect the resulting changes.

Table 6-1. How a Bill Becomes a Law, *continued*

Legislative Action	Documents Produced
The bill is read a third time in the house of origin, explained by the author, discussed in that house, and voted on by roll call vote.	Debates are not published. *Journals* provide a record of the proceedings. However, they record only the votes.
Once the bill is approved by the house of origin, it goes to the second house, where the same process of consideration is repeated. There are three routes for the bill to become law: approval by the second house in the same form; approval by the second house in amended form, which the first house accepts; or approval by the second house in amended form that the first house rejects, resulting in a conference committee.	The *Journal* notes the passage of the bill and its return to the house of origin.
If the bill passes the second house, it is returned to the house of origin with a message that it was passed.	The bill is **enrolled**, meaning it is printed in its final form with blanks for signatures of legislative officers, the governor, and the secretary of state. The **digest** is omitted from this printing.
If the second house amends the bill, the house of origin must agree with the amendments, which is called concurrence.	Following **concurrence**, the bill is **enrolled**.
If the house of origin does not approve the amended version, the two houses may appoint a conference committee to draft an agreed version. If the conference committee reaches agreement, the bill is returned to both houses for a vote.	Once the agreed bill is passed by both houses, it is **enrolled**.
The enrolled bill is sent to the governor. The governor can sign the bill, let it become law without signature, or veto the bill.	The governor's action is reported in the **Daily History**.
An enacted bill is "chaptered" as a session law, meaning that it is assigned a chapter number in *Statutes and Amendments to the Codes.* Later the new statute is codified in one of California's 29 codes.	A **chapter number** is merely a chronological record of when the bill was enacted. The **codification number** places the new statute with others on related topics.

ing only, while others will be useful for both processes. The publications for the current year can be viewed at www.leginfo.ca.gov/legpubs.html.[5] Publications from past years can be found on microform in a library or in hard copy at the California State Archives in Sacramento.

A **Daily File** is produced by both the Assembly and the Senate. It lists current officers, the Order of Business, a tentative schedule for the entire legislative session, and a schedule of bills to be read on the floor and during committee hearings.

The **Legislative Index** is a subject-matter index of all bills being considered in the current legislative session, published by the Legislative Counsel. This index includes not only bills, but also proposed constitutional amendments, and concurrent and joint resolutions. For purposes of legislative history research, be aware that if the subject of a particular bill changes during the legislative process, the original subject is not removed from the Legislative Index.[6]

The **Table of Sections Affected** is also published by the Legislative Counsel. It provides a cumulative listing of each section of the California Constitution, the codes, and uncodified laws affected by measures that are introduced in the legislature.

The Senate and the Assembly each produces a **Daily Journal**. It is the daily, official record of business that has been transacted in each house. The **Senate Daily Journal** includes the title of each measure

---

5. For a detailed introduction to the legislative process in California, see Chapter 9 of *California's Legislature*, a book published by the Office of the Assembly Chief Clerk. The contents of the book can be viewed online at www.leginfo.ca.gov/legpubs.html. Click on "California's Legislature" to view the book.

6. Members of the legislature may introduce only a limited number of bills in the course of a single session and must introduce most of them before the end of February. *See* California Legislature Jt. R. 54, at www.leginfo.ca.gov/rules/joint_rules.html. In order not to lose the opportunity to introduce legislation on a particular topic after the February deadline, legislators often introduce bills with "dummy" subjects, which are then entered in the index. When the bill is amended by changing the subject completely, the original "dummy" subject remains in the index.

the Senate considered, results of floor votes, messages from the governor and the Assembly, and reports from Senate committees of their deliberations on pending legislation. The **Assembly Daily Journal** shows all roll call votes, lists bill introductions, and records other official Assembly actions. At the end of the session, each *Journal* is bound in book form.

Each house produces a **Daily History** at the end of each day's session. The Daily History lists specific actions taken on legislation, listed in numerical order. At the end of the week, the Daily History is accumulated into a **Weekly History**. Similarly, at the end of the legislative session, the Weekly Histories are compiled into a **Final History** that shows the disposition of all measures introduced during that session.[7]

III. California Bill Tracking

Each year, California legislators introduce a large number of bills that may or may not be enacted into law. These bills may affect the rights of a client by proposing new laws or amending existing laws. In order to advise a client correctly, an attorney needs to identify new bills that could affect the client's interests and follow their progress through the legislative process. This bill tracking can easily be done online on the official site for California legislative information that is maintained by the Legislative Counsel, the California Legislature's nonpartisan legal counsel. The Legislative Counsel helps draft legislation, prepares a digest for each bill, and advises the legislature on the constitutionality and effect of proposed legislation. See Table 6-2 for an outline of the process for bill tracking online.

---

7. Final Histories for both the Senate and the Assembly and *Journals* of each house can be found online at http://192.234.213.35/clerkarchive. Both Final Histories and *Journals* may be available in your library in print.

Table 6-2. Outline for Bill Tracking Online

1. Go to the California Legislative Counsel's website at www.leginfo.ca.gov.
2. Click on "Bill Information."
3. Click on the current session, for example, "(2007–2008)CURRENT."
4. Choose whether you want to search for Senate bills, Assembly bills, or both.
5. Choose one of three options to search by:
   a. Bill Number or
   b. Author(s) or
   c. Keyword(s)
6. Choose the correct bill from the resulting list.

A. Researching with a Bill Number

If you know the number of a bill, you can track it by going to the Legislative Counsel's website at www.leginfo.ca.gov and clicking on "Bill Information."[8] You can search on the "Bill Information" page by bill number, author, or keyword. Simply click on "Bill Number," enter the number in the box, and click on "Search."

The resulting listing will include every bill with that number. For example, if the bill you are tracking is Assembly Bill 33, typing "AB33" into the query box will bring up all bills with the number "33."[9] The list could include an Assembly Constitutional Amendment (ACA) and an Assembly Joint Resolution (AJR), as well as the bill you want. Simply

---

8. Similar searches can be conducted on the Senate and Assembly websites, www.senate.ca.gov and www.assembly.ca.gov, from the "Legislation" links.

9. According to the Joint Rules of the Senate and Assembly, the term "bills" includes house, concurrent, and joint resolutions and constitutional amendments, as well as proposed legislation. E. Dotson Wilson & Brian S. Ebbert, *California's Legislature* 110 (Office of the Assembly Chief Clerk 2006) (available at www.leginfo.ca.gov/pdf/Ch_09_CaLegi06.pdf).

click on the link for the bill to get a listing of all documents associated with it. The documents can be viewed in either HTML or PDF format.

B. Other Approaches to Bill Tracking

1. Legislative Counsel Resources

If you do not know the bill number, you can search on the same page of the Legislative Counsel's website by author or by keyword. From the "Bill Information" page, typing in either the authors or the keywords of the bill title will lead you to a list of bills to choose from. Additionally, the "Bill Information" page contains a hyperlink to an "Index," which lists all bills introduced in both chambers during the legislative session. The bills are sorted by bill number and by author.

You can also track a pending bill by consulting the Daily File for both houses, which you can access by clicking on the hyperlink for "Legislative WWW Sites" and then clicking on "Daily File" in the websites for both houses.

Another approach is to consult the Legislative Index, at www.leginfo.ca.gov/legpubs.html, which was mentioned in Part II above. This index is organized by subject matter and is published by the Legislative Counsel. However, as noted above, this index does not indicate when subject matter is removed from a bill during the legislative process. The Legislative Counsel also provides a Table of Sections Affected, which you can use to see if existing statutes relating to your client's interests will potentially be affected by pending legislation. The index is available in California depository libraries and is sold in Sacramento by the Legislative Bill Room.

2. Audio and Video Resources

Another possible way to track pending legislation is by listening to audio tapes or watching video broadcasts or tapes of committee hearings. For the most part, the Assembly audiotapes only, while the Senate both audio and video records some sessions and committee hearings. Notice of taped hearings can be found on both the Senate and the Assembly websites, and many Senate and some Assembly hearings are available on the California Channel; check the California Channel website at www.calchannel.com.

3. Print Resources

You can keep up with newly enacted legislation in print sources by consulting either *Deering's Advance Legislative Service* or *West's California Legislative Service*. Both of these services consist of softbound pamphlets that are published at regular intervals throughout the year. They both include chaptered laws (enacted laws that have not yet been inserted in the codes) and state court rule amendments, as well as lists of code sections affected by new legislation. *West's California Legislative Service* also includes proposed constitutional amendments and ballot propositions.

IV. California Legislative History Research

A. In General

Lawyers conduct legislative history research when the meaning of a statute is not clear from the text or context of the statute. Legislative history research is especially useful for new legislation that has not yet been interpreted by the courts. When a statute is ambiguous, reviewing the documents created in the course of enacting the statute can assist in determining the legislature's intent. When litigation involves a statute whose meaning is arguably unclear, first look to see if courts have already interpreted the statute. If not, you will need to turn to legislative history and refer to it in your briefs to the court.

Legislative history research is the reverse of bill tracking. Bill tracking follows the legislative process forward from the introduction of a bill; legislative history research follows the legislative process backward from the enacted statute. Therefore, many of the sources you would consult in their current editions for bill tracking will also be necessary for legislative history research, but this time for past years. From the statute as it appears in either *Deering's California Codes Annotated* or *West's Annotated California Codes*, you can follow the statute's legislative history through the session law chapter number, then the bill number, and finally the documents produced by the legislative process.

This part explains the sources of legislative history in California and how to conduct legislative history research. Some information is available locally in print and microfilm, and most information for statutes passed after January 1, 1993, is available online through the state website. For some statutes, however, you will need to go to the California State Archives in Sacramento[10] or check with the Chief Clerk of the State Assembly or the California State Library, also in Sacramento. As an alternative, practicing attorneys may instead rely on commercial services that conduct legislative history research for a fee.[11]

B. Researching the Legislative History of a California Statute

Table 6-3 outlines the steps needed to research the legislative history of a California statute. As an example, suppose you have learned of a statute that assesses a fine for leaving a child six years old or younger unsupervised in a car under certain circumstances. The statute is codified at Cal. Veh. Code § 15620. The statutory language says that those circumstances include "conditions that pre-

---

10. The California State Archives is located at 1020 "O" Street in Sacramento. The phone number is (916) 653-7715 or (916) 653-2246. The website is at www.ss.ca.gov/archives; however, the Archives does not provide a digital archive on the website.

11. The leading commercial services are Legislative Intent Service, www.legintent.com; Legislative Research Incorporated, www.lrihistory.com; and Legislative History & Legislative Intent, www.lhclearinghouse.com.

Table 6-3. Outline for Legislative History Research in California

1. Review the history note following a published statute to learn the original bill number.
2. Gather background information by locating the citation to the statute in *Statutes and Amendments to the Codes.*
3. Read the Legislative Counsel's Digest, printed at the beginning of the session law.
4. Review the text of the bill and all proposed amendments to the original text.
5. Read any available committee staff Bill Analyses.
6. Read the Legislative Counsel Opinion, if one is available.
7. Look at Letters of Intent, if available.
8. Read the Governor's Signing Statement, if available.
9. Read any relevant material in the "Review of Selected California Legislation," published by the *McGeorge Law Review.*

sent a significant risk to the child's health or safety," but it does not define what those conditions are. It is possible that researching the legislative history of the statute will give you more information.

1. Find the Original Bill Number

Legislative history research starts with the enacted statute, which can be found in both *West's* and *Deering's California Codes Annotated* and online through LexisNexis or Westlaw. At the end of the statutory language, the publisher provides a note that gives the history of the statute. Often the note is placed in brackets or parentheses to distinguish it from the text of the statute. This note includes a reference to the chaptered session law number, the date for the code section, and the original bill number. The original bill number for Cal. Veh. Code § 15620 was SB 255; it was enacted in 2001.

2. Gather Session Law Information

The next step is to find the appropriate volume of *Statutes and Amendments to the Codes*,[12] the compilation of all "chaptered" bills enacted in each two-year session of the legislature. A bill is "chaptered" after it has been enacted and is sent to the secretary of state's office; these compiled enacted laws are called "session laws." Session laws print statutes in the form in which they were enacted by the legislature and in the chronological order in which they were enacted. Each new law is assigned a "chapter" number, which simply indicates the chronological order in which it was enacted. Either use the bill number you found in the annotated code, or search the Table of Laws Enacted in volume 1 of *Statutes and Amendments to the Codes* for that year or the Summary Digest in the final volume for the year to find the bill number. Senate bill numbers are preceded by "SB," while Assembly bill numbers are preceded by "AB."

3. Read the Legislative Counsel's Digest

At the beginning of the session law, you will see the bill digest. The Legislative Counsel creates the digest and attaches it to each bill when it is first printed, immediately after the sponsor introduces the bill. The digest follows the bill through all its versions and is amended to reflect amendments to the bill. The version of the digest you see in the session law reflects the final text of the statute. Before 1999, this digest tended merely to list other code sections affected by this bill. Since 1999, the digest has become more descriptive of the contents and purpose of the bill, so more recent digests will be much more useful for legislative history research.

The session law may also include uncodified legislative intent language that does not become part of the statute itself. In the case of

---

12. Both the *ALWD Citation Manual* and the *Bluebook* refer to this publication as *Statutes of California*, but the text itself and California librarians refer to it as *Statutes and Amendments to the Codes*.

SB 255, which became Cal. Veh. Code § 15620, the uncodified language tells you that the legislature was concerned about a "child's access to the vehicle's controls" and the "exposure of the child to extreme cold or heat." These concerns can be useful to you in determining the legislative intent behind this statute.[13]

4. Review the Bill's Text and Proposed Amendments

Next, review all of the versions of the bill as it passed through the legislative process. For statutes enacted after January 1, 1993, all of the versions can be found through the Legislative Counsel's website at www.leginfo.ca.gov. Click on "Bill Information" and enter the legislative session by date and the bill number and click "Search." The result will be a page titled "Bill Documents." It provides a list of all versions of the bill's text from its introduction until it was chaptered, as well as the final "History" of the bill. (The final history of SB 255 is set out in Appendix 6-A of this chapter.)

From this website, you can print the bill texts in HTML or PDF format. In looking through the versions, note that deletions are indicated by strike-outs and additions are indicated with italics. For statutes enacted before 1993, LexisNexis and Westlaw have the texts of bills and amendments dating back to 1991. For statutes before 1991, you will have to consult microfiche in a law library or go to the State Archives in Sacramento.

5. Read the Bill Analysis

Each time a bill is considered by a Senate or Assembly committee, or is presented on the floor of either house, the staff prepares a bill analysis. These analyses can be another source of finding legislative

---

13. The uncodified legislative intent language for this statute also appears in the editorial materials following the statute in *West's California Codes Annotated*. It does not appear in *Deering's California Codes Annotated*.

intent, and you should consult them next. The bill analyses for statutes enacted after 1992 can be found on the Legislative Counsel's website; LexisNexis and Westlaw include committee analyses from 1991 forward. Before that date, the only source is the State Archives.

A bill analysis includes a description of the proposed statute, its relation to existing law, actions already taken in the committee and in the other legislative house, and an analysis of the bill. The analysis may include a discussion of the author's purpose in introducing the bill and arguments in support of and opposition to the bill. It may raise issues that the staff sees presented by the text of the bill.

To continue our example, the bill analysis prepared for the Assembly Committee on Transportation noted as an area of concern in relation to Cal. Veh. Code § 15620 that the "significant risk" standard was "vague for lack of definition." (Excerpts from this analysis are provided in Appendix 6-B of this chapter.)

6. Read Any Legislative Counsel Opinion

Another source of legislative history is a Legislative Counsel Opinion. A legislator may ask the legislative counsel to interpret proposed legislation; very few bills have Legislative Counsel Opinions attached to them. There are two possible sources you can check. *West's Annotated California Codes* prints some Legislative Counsel Opinions in the editorial material immediately following the text of the statute. This is the easiest place to look. *Deering's California Codes Annotated* does not include these interpretations. The other place to look for these opinions is in the *Journal of the Assembly* or the *Journal of the Senate.* Look in the indexes of each *Journal* under "Legislative Counsel, opinions of" or similar language. Not all Legislative Counsel Opinions are printed in the *Journals.*

7. Other Sources for California Legislative History

Three final sources of legislative history are available. The first is a letter of intent that the legislature may provide when it sends the bill to the governor for signing. Letters of intent may be printed in the *Journals* of the Senate or Assembly, and they may be included in the author's file and the governor's file at the State Archives.

Another possible source of legislative history is a signing statement by the governor. These statements will also be available in the governor's file at the State Archives or may be found on the governor's website at http://gov.ca.gov.

Finally, one very accessible source of legislative history is the annual "Review of Selected California Legislation" published annually by the *McGeorge Law Review* (previously the *Pacific Law Journal*) since 1970. Continuing our example, if you consulted volume 33 of the *McGeorge Law Review*, you would find the bill's author intentionally left the "significant risk" language undefined to allow police officers greater latitude when deciding if the law has been violated.[14]

V. Initiative and Referendum in California[15]

Legislation in California can also come directly from the people in the form of the initiative and referendum processes, discussed in Chapter 4 on the California Constitution. There are four required steps for members of the public to put an initiative on the ballot. The first step is writing the initiative, which proponents can do themselves. They can also get help from the Legislative Counsel's office. The second step is to get a title and a summary of the chief purpose

---

14. Jaeson D. White, Student Author, *Sit Right Here Honey, I'll Be Right Back: The Unattended Child in Motor Vehicle Safety Act*, 33 McGeorge L. Rev. 343, 350 (2001–2002).

15. This description of the initiative and referendum process is taken largely from the "2002 Initiative Guide" found on the website of the California Secretary of State at www.sos.ca.gov/elections/init_guide.htm.

of the initiative from the attorney general. If the attorney general determines that the proposed legislation would have a fiscal impact, the Department of Finance and the Joint Legislative Budget Committee must together prepare an analysis of that impact. The third step is the one that most California residents are familiar with: circulation of the initiative petition to collect voter signatures. The number of signatures for a statutory initiative must equal at least 5% of the total votes cast for governor in the most recent gubernatorial election. Signatures for a constitutional initiative must equal at least 8% of the total votes cast for governor in the last gubernatorial election. The final step is filing the signatures with the appropriate county elections official, who must then verify the signatures to assure that they represent the registered voters in that county. Once certified, the measure is sent to the California Legislature. Each house assigns the measure to the appropriate committees, which hold joint public hearings. However, the legislature cannot amend the initiative or prevent it from appearing on the ballot.

Voters may also approve or reject legislation adopted by the California Legislature through the referendum process. Although the system is similar to that used for initiatives, there is an important timing difference. Referenda petitions must be circulated within 90 days of enactment of the bill that is being referred. Initiatives need be qualified by collecting the required number of signatures at least 131 days before the election.

You can track initiatives and referenda as they progress from initial proposal to certification on the California Secretary of State's website at www.sos.ca.gov. Click on "Ballot Measures" and then on "Initiative Update."

VI. Federal Legislative Research

Researching the federal legislative process involves roughly the same steps as researching California's laws, though some of the terminology is different. The United States Congress meets for two-year sessions, beginning on January 3 following a national election in November. Each session is divided into two terms, one for each year.

Bills are numbered sequentially in each chamber of Congress. Generally, Senate bill numbers are preceded by an "S," and House bill numbers are preceded by "H.R." for "House Resolution." When a federal statute is enacted, it is printed as a *slip law* and assigned a *public law number*. This number is in the form Pub. L. No. 107–110, where the numerals before the hyphen represent the two-year Congressional session in which the statute was enacted and the numerals after the hyphen are assigned chronologically. The public law number given above is for the No Child Left Behind Act, which was passed in 2002 during the 107th Congress.

The new statute is later published as a *session law* in a series called *United States Statutes at Large*, which is the federal counterpart of *Statutes and Amendments to the Codes* in California. Session laws are designated by volume and page number in *Statutes at Large*, e.g., 115 Stat. 1425. Finally, the statute is assigned a *statute number* when it is codified with statutes having similar topics in the *United States Code*. The citation for the first section of the No Child Left Behind Act is 20 U.S.C. §6301.

A. Federal Bill Tracking

More Congressional material is available daily via the Internet, and using Internet sources for bill tracking is often easier than using print sources. The Library of Congress site at http://thomas.loc.gov provides bill summaries and status, committee reports, and the *Congressional Record* (which records debate in the House and Senate). The Government Printing Office site at www.gpoaccess.gov contains bills, selected hearings and reports, and the *Congressional Record*. Coverage varies even within a single site, so check carefully.

B. Federal Legislative History

As with California legislative history, federal legislative history research begins with the statute number. If you do not know the statute number, use an annotated code to find it (as described in Chapter 5). With a statute number, you can find the session law citation and public law number following the text of the statute, which will lead to the legislative history of the bill as it worked its way through Congress.

1. Sources of Federal Legislative History

In conducting federal legislative history research, you are looking for sources that are often very different from the sources available for California legislative history research. Federal legislative history is found in committee reports, materials from committee hearings, and transcripts of floor debates, none of which exist in California. Congressional committee reports are often lengthy documents that contain the committee's analysis of the bill, the reasons for enacting it, and the views of any members who disagreed with those reasons. Congressional hearing materials include transcripts from the proceedings as well as documents such as prepared testimony and exhibits. These documents may be available in local federal depository libraries, but not all libraries are likely to have all reports and hearing materials.

Unlike the *Journal of the Senate* and the *Journal of the Assembly* in California, which print only records of votes without any transcripts of debates, the *Congressional Record* publishes transcripts of floor debates in the Senate and House of Representatives. Be wary of relying on these debates, however, as it is impossible to know which legislators were present during the debate to hear the remarks. In addition, members of Congress may not actually have delivered their remarks in person; members can amend their remarks and even submit written statements that are published in transcript form as if they were spoken.

Table 6-4. Selected Sources for Federal Legislative History in Print

Source	Contents
United States Code Congressional and Administrative News (USCCAN)	Selected reprints and excerpts of committee reports; references to other reports and to the *Congressional Record*
Congressional Information Service (CIS)	Full text of bills, committee reports, and hearings on microfiche; print indexes and abstracts in bound volumes
Congressional Record	Debate from the floor of the House and Senate

2. Compiled Legislative History

Researchers have compiled legislative history for certain federal statutes that researchers or lawyers consider important. Two reference books that identify legislative histories of major federal statutes are *Sources of Compiled Legislative Histories*[16] and *Federal Legislative Histories*.[17]

3. Print Sources for Federal Legislative History

Table 6-4 contains the most common print sources for researching federal legislative history. Some of them contain a "How to Use" section at the beginning; otherwise, consult a reference librarian or one of the texts noted in the bibliography at the end of this book.

---

16. Nancy P. Johnson, *Sources of Compiled Legislative Histories: A Bibliography of Government Documents, Periodical Articles, and Books* (AALL 2000).

17. Bernard D. Reams, Jr., *Federal Legislative Histories: An Annotated Bibliography and Index to Officially Published Sources* (Greenwood Press 1994).

4. Online Sources for Federal Legislative History

The sites noted earlier in this chapter for tracking federal legislation also provide useful information for legislative history research. The Library of Congress site at http://thomas.loc.gov provides bill summaries and status, committee reports, and the *Congressional Record*. The Government Printing Office site at www.gpoaccess.gov contains bills, selected hearings and reports, and the *Congressional Record*.

Appendix 6-A. Final Bill History

This is the history of SB 255, which was enacted in 2001. The history is taken from the Office of Legislative Counsel website at www.leginfo.ca.gov/pub/01-02/bill/sen/sb_0251-0300/sb_255_bill _20011013_history.html.

```
COMPLETE BILL HISTORY

BILL NUMBER: S.B. No. 255

AUTHOR: Speier

TOPIC: Crimes: unattended children in vehicles.

TYPE OF BILL:    Inactive
                 Non-Urgency
                 Non-Appropriations
                 Majority Vote Required
                 State-Mandated Local Program
                 Fiscal
                 Non-Tax Levy

BILL HISTORY

2001

Oct. 13         Chaptered by Secretary of State.
                Chapter 855, Statutes of 2001.

Oct. 12         Approved by Governor.

Sept. 19        Enrolled. To Governor at 3 p.m.

Sept. 12        Senate concurs in Assembly amendments.
                (Ayes 24. Noes 11. Page 2815.) To
                enrollment.

Sept. 5         In Senate. To unfinished business.

Sept. 5         Read third time. Passed. (Ayes 53.
                Noes 17. Page 3456.) To Senate.

Aug. 31         Read second time. To third reading.

Aug. 30         From committee: Do pass as amended.
                (Ayes 13. Noes 3.) Read second time.
                Amended. To second reading.
```

Aug. 22	From committee with author's amendments. Read second time. Amended. Re-referred to committee.
July 16	Read second time. Amended. Re-referred to Com. on APPR.
July 14	From committee: Do pass as amended, but first amend, and re-refer to Com. on APPR. (Ayes 13. Noes 2.)
July 2	From committee with author's amendments. Read second time. Amended. Re-referred to committee.
June 25	To Com. on TRANS.
June 6	In Assembly. Read first time. Held at Desk.
June 6	Read third time. Passed. (Ayes 26. Noes 10. Page 1468.) To Assembly.
June 5	Read third time. Amended. To third reading.
May 25	Read second time. Amended. To third reading.
May 24	From committee: Do pass as amended. (Ayes 8. Noes 3. Page 1217.)
May 22	Set for hearing May 24.
May 16	Hearing postponed by committee.
May 15	Set for hearing May 21.
May 14	Set, first hearing. Hearing canceled at the request of author.
May 7	Set for hearing May 14.
May 3	From committee with author's amendments. Read second time. Amended. Re-referred to committee.
Apr. 30	Read second time. Amended. Re-referred to Com. on APPR.
Apr. 26	From committee: Do pass as amended, but first amend, and re-refer to Com. on APPR. (Ayes 5. Noes 0. Page 657.)

Apr. 5	From committee with author's amendments. Read second time. Amended. Re-referred to committee.
Mar. 12	Set, first hearing. Hearing canceled at the request of author. Set for hearing April 17.
Mar. 5	Set for hearing April 3.
Mar. 1	To Com. on PUB. S.
Feb. 16	From print. May be acted upon on or after March 18.
Feb. 15	Introduced. Read first time. To Com. on RLS. for assignment. To print.

Appendix 6-B. Bill Analysis

The following excerpt is taken from seven pages of analysis produced by the Assembly Committee on Transportation as it considered SB 255. Lengthy omissions are indicated by asterisks. The full committee analysis is available at www.leginfo.ca.gov/pub/01-02/bill/sen/sb_0251-0300/sb_255_cfa_20010706_143350_asm_comm.html.

```
BILL ANALYSIS
255                                                    SB
                                                   Page A
          ASSEMBLY COMMITTEE ON TRANSPORTATION
                   John Dutra, Chair
      SB 255 (Speier) - As Amended: July 2, 2001


SENATE VOTE: 26—10

SUBJECT: Crimes: unattended children in vehicles

SUMMARY: Makes it an infraction to leave a child
under the age of six unattended in a motor vehicle,
as specified, and creates a fund for an educational
campaign regarding the dangers of leaving a child in
a vehicle. Specifically, this bill:

1)Creates the "Unattended Child in Motor Vehicle
Safety Act" and contains intent language stating that
it is the purpose of this division of the Vehicle
Code to help prevent injuries to, and the death of,
young children from the effects of being left alone
in a motor vehicle, to help educate parents and care-
takers about the dangers of leaving children alone in
a motor vehicle, and to authorize a monetary fine to
be imposed on a person for leaving a young child
alone in a motor vehicle in circumstances that pose a
life safety risk.

***

2)Provides that the "Unattended Child in Motor Vehi-
cle Safety Act" shall be known and cited as "Kait-
lyn's Law."
```

EXISTING LAW makes it a crime for any person, under circumstances or conditions likely to produce great bodily harm or death, to willfully cause or permit any child to suffer, or inflict thereon, unjustifiable physical pain or mental suffering, or having the care or custody of any child, to willfully cause or permit the person or health of that child to be injured, or willfully cause or permit that child to be placed in a situation where his or her person or health is endangered. This crime is punishable by imprisonment in a county jail not exceeding one year, or in the state prison for two, four, or six years. Existing law also provides that no person shall leave standing a locked vehicle in which there is any person who cannot readily escape therefrom and that doing so constitutes an infraction.

FISCAL EFFECT: According to the Senate Appropriations Committee, the bill appears to redirect 60% of state penalties, county penalties and other penalties and assessments that otherwise would go according to statutory allocation for various purposes.

COMMENTS: This bill is premised on the belief that an educational campaign approach directed at social ills does not work unless it is coupled with an enforcement component.

***

Areas of Concern:

1)Most cases involving unattended children in vehicles occur on private property, such as parking lots and driveways. Law enforcement agencies might not have jurisdiction in such areas and, therefore, would be unable to cite for violation of this new law.

2)The first standard triggering the application of this new law (conditions that present a significant risk to the child's health and safety) is vague for lack of definition.

***

Analysis Prepared by: Joseph Furtado / TRANS. / (916) 319—2093

Chapter 7

Administrative Law

I. Administrative Law and Governmental Agencies

Administrative law is primary authority like constitutions, statutes, and cases. It differs from those primary authorities because it issues from the executive branch. Administrative law includes both regulations and adjudicatory decisions of governmental agencies. California defines state agencies to include "every state office, officer, department, division, bureau, board, and commission."[1] The online directory of state agencies lists over 500 state agencies, ranging from the Department of Alcoholic Beverage Control to the Workforce Investment Board.[2]

While agencies are generally part of the executive branch, the source of their authority is an *enabling statute* passed by the legislature. In addition, some California agencies are created, or their creation is authorized, by the state constitution or by voter initiative. The constitution created, for example, the Public Utilities Commission.[3] Such agencies are designated "constitutional agencies," and the usual rules of administrative law do not apply to them. Other agencies may be created by voter initiative. For ex-

---

1. Cal. Govt. Code Ann. § 11000 (Lexis 1997).

2. The State Agencies Directory can be found at www.ca.gov/About/Government/agencyindex.html. Not all of the state agencies listed exercise all the functions discussed below. Although all of these bodies qualify as "state agencies," the California Code of Regulations (CCR) currently includes regulations from only 182 agencies.

3. *See* Cal. Const. art. XII.

ample, in 1984 a voter initiative amended the California Constitution to authorize the California State Lottery and enacted the California State Lottery Act of 1984.[4] That act created the Lottery Commission, the agency that operates the lottery.[5] The statutory and constitutional provisions that create agencies establish the powers and duties of the agencies. Each agency must work within the limits set by its enabling statute; all actions taken and regulations issued by an agency that exceed the powers granted in the enabling statute are void.[6]

Unlike other parts of the government, administrative agencies can perform all three governmental functions. Agencies exercise a legislative function when they promulgate regulations that interpret and apply statutes; these regulations are similar in form and have similar authority to statutes. In fact, California regulations are often referred to as "quasi-legislative rules." Agencies are part of the executive branch of the government, so they also exercise executive authority. Examples of this authority are licensing people to practice professions, such as architecture and cosmetology, and conducting investigations to see whether laws are being followed, such as anti-poaching operations by the Department of Fish and Game. Agencies also hold quasi-judicial hearings to decide application of the agency's rules in specific cases, such as denial of government benefits. These hearings are similar to court proceedings, but are less formal.

In general, agencies function within the bounds of an Administrative Procedure Act (APA). California's APA can be found in the Government Code at sections 11340–11365. Some agencies and the actions of some agencies are exempt from the APA under sections

---

4. *See* Cal. Const. art. IV, § 19, subd. (d); Cal. Govt. Code §§ 8880–8880.72 (Lexis 2005 & Supp. 2008); *see also* November 1984 Voter Information Guide for Proposition 37, at http://traynor.uchastings.edu.

5. Cal. Govt. Code Ann. § 8880.15. Be sure to research the enabling statute for all agencies, including those authorized by the California Constitution or a voter initiative.

6. *See Morris v. Williams*, 67 Cal. 2d 733, 433 P.2d 697, 63 Cal. Rptr. 689 (1967).

11351–11361, although these exemptions have their own exceptions written into them.[7] These exemptions and exceptions apply, for example, to California's Public Utilities Commission, Division of Workers' Compensation, State Water Resources Control Board, and Lottery Commission.

Each of the three branches of government has some oversight of agency actions. The legislative branch establishes agency powers and can add to them or remove them with later legislation. The legislative branch also provides operating funds to agencies. The courts determine in contested cases whether agencies' operations and rules are authorized by their enabling acts. The governor supervises all state agencies, and the executive branch exercises control over many agencies by appointing their highest officials.

II. Administrative Regulations

The California APA establishes not only the procedures for adopting, amending, and appealing agency regulations, but also the Office of Administrative Law (OAL) in the executive branch. The functions of the OAL are to make sure that citizens can understand the regulations as written, that regulations are authorized by statute, and that they are consistent with other law. All proposed regulations must be approved by the OAL before they are filed with the Secretary of State's office, and the OAL can disapprove proposed regulations.[8]

All regulations are subject to the APA's rulemaking procedures. A regulation is "every rule, regulation, order, or standard of general application or amendment, supplement, or revision of any rule, regulation, order, or standard adopted by any state agency to implement, interpret, or make specific the law enforced or administered by it, or

---

7. Additional exemptions can be found in section 11340.9.

8. Agencies can appeal these disapprovals to the governor. A link to the governor's resulting decisions can by found on the OAL website at www.oal.ca.gov.

Table 7-1. Example of the Relationship between Statutes and Regulations

Statute: Because of the importance of agriculture to the California economy, the legislature enacted a law addressing "Certification, Processing and Canning, and Canned Foods." Under the terms of the statute, the Department of Food and Agriculture, an agency, was directed to establish standards for processing various agricultural products, including tomatoes.

Regulation: A regulation issued by the Department of Food and Agriculture specifies that "Any load of tomatoes which is offered for delivery to a canner shall be rejected and turned back to the grower if in excess of 2 percent, by weight, is affected by worm damage. A tomato is scoreable for worm damage when a worm has penetrated the flesh."

Sources: Cal. Food & Agric. Code Ann. § 40761(a) (Lexis 1997); Cal. Code Regs. tit. 3, § 1332.1 (2007).

to govern its procedure."[9] Or, as the OAL itself says, "If a rule looks like a regulation, reads like a regulation, and acts like a regulation, it will be treated by the courts as a regulation whether or not the issuing agency so labeled it."[10]

Agencies promulgate regulations to implement a statute, to interpret a statute, or to make a statute specific. Agencies are the "experts" in the field, so the legislature leaves to the agency the task of supplying the details that the legislature is not able to include in the more general statute. (See Table 7-1.) Regulations may also provide guidance based on an agency's understanding of a relevant statute or determine procedural deadlines and format for agency filings.

Once a regulation is promulgated, it is published in the California Code of Regulations (CCR), which is divided into titles. The ti-

---

9. Cal. Govt. Code Ann. § 11342.600 (Lexis Supp. 2008).
10. Office of Administrative Law, *What Is a Regulation?* 2 (April 6, 2006) (available at www.oal.ca.gov/publications.htm).

Table 7-2. California Code of Regulations Titles

Titles

1. General Provisions	15. Crime Prevention and Corrections
2. Administration	
3. Food and Agriculture	16. Professional and Vocational
4. Business Regulations	17. Public Health
5. Education	18. Public Revenues
6. Governor [no regulations filed]	19. Public Safety
7. Harbors and Navigation	20. Public Utilities and Energy
8. Industrial Relations	21. Public Works
9. Rehabilitative and Developmental Service	22. Social Security
	23. Water
10. Investment	24. Building Standards*
11. Law	25. Housing and Community
12. Military and Veterans Affairs	26. Toxics
13. Motor Vehicles	27. Environmental Protection
14. Natural Resources	28. Managed Health Care

* Title 24 is now published by the California Building Standards Commission. The Commission republishes Title 24 in its entirety every three years. It is available in print, and some parts are available online at the Commission's website at www.bsc.ca.gov.

tles are then subdivided in an outline format that may include divisions, chapters, subchapters, groups, subgroups, articles, and sections, although a division may use only some of these subdivisions. Regardless of the outline format chosen, the sections within a particular title are numbered consecutively from 1 to the highest number. Hence, the regulation discussed in Table 7-1 can be found in Title 3 at § 1332.1. (See Table 7-2 for a list of the titles of the Code of Regulations.)

Although regulations and statutes are both primary authority, regulations are subordinate to statutes. In any inconsistency between a regulation and a statute, the statute has priority.

III. Researching California Administrative Regulations

The process for researching California administrative law is outlined in Table 7-3 and explained in detail below.

Table 7-3. Outline for California Administrative Law Research

1. Find the statutory or constitutional provision granting the agency power to act.
2. Research case law to determine whether the agency acted within that power.
3. Find the text of the relevant regulation in the California Code of Regulations (CCR).
4. Update the rule in the *California Regulatory Notice Register* ("Z Register") to find any proposed changes.
5. Find agency and judicial decisions applying the rule in similar circumstances.

A. Underground Regulations

Given the expansive definition of a regulation cited above, it may seem impossible for an agency to believe any action with general applicability would not qualify as a "regulation." However, California agencies have routinely created policies or procedures that they believe do not have to be promulgated as regulations using the procedures established in the APA. These agency actions are referred to as "underground regulations," and they cannot be enforced legally. If you think an agency has taken an action against your client based on what you believe to be an underground regulation, you can challenge the underground regulation by filing a petition with the OAL, which will issue an advisory opinion, referred to as a "determination." Should the OAL determine that an underground regulation is involved, you can then ask a court to enjoin enforcement of the underground regulation.[11]

B. Researching the Enabling Act

Assuming you are dealing with a properly promulgated regulation, the initial question analytically is whether the agency acted within its power. If that is in doubt, your first step in researching a regulation is to find the statute (or the constitutional provision) that gives the agency power to act.[12] The next step is to find cases that interpret those provisions. This research will help determine whether the agency acted within the limits of its power in the situation that affects your client. Chapters 4 and 5 explain the process of researching the California statutory codes to find constitutional provisions and statutes as well as annotations to relevant cases. Chapter 3 explains how to find additional cases using reporters and digests. If the agency's power is clear, skip this inquiry and move directly to finding relevant regulations, as explained below.

C. California Code of Regulations

The Office of Administrative Law is charged with publishing all California regulations in the California Code of Regulations (CCR). The OAL has licensed publication of both print and electronic versions of the Code to Thomson West. The print version is *Barclays Official California Code of Regulations* ("*Barclays*"). *Barclays* is published in three-ring binders; some titles have only one binder, while others may cover as many as four. *Barclays* includes the full text of all promulgated regulations. It is updated weekly through the *California Regulatory Code*

---

11. Section 11350(a) of the APA authorizes any interested person to bring an action for a declaratory judgment to test the validity of a regulation.

12. Although this step comes first analytically, it may be more efficient to find the regulation first and look at the authority citation following the text of the regulation. See the discussion of the CCR below.

Supplement (the "*Supplement*"). The *Supplement* is identified by reference to the *California Regulatory Notice Register*, which is discussed below. Each issue of the *Supplement* is identified by *Register* year and weekly issue number, i.e., *Register* 2007, No. 30. The *Supplement* consists of insert pages for the binders. The "Filing Instructions" for each issue of the *Supplement* should be located in the Title 1 binder; check the date of the most recent *Supplement* in your library's *Barclays* to find out how recent your pages are. Finally, *Barclays* includes a *Digest of New Regulations* (the "*Digest*") that can help you keep track of regulatory research and past regulatory developments. Your library will most likely keep the *Digest* issues filed with the *Barclays* binders in separate binders or other holders.

Researching California regulations in print is relatively straightforward. *Barclays* includes a "Master Index," which is published in its own binder and is usually shelved at the end of the entire series. It is divided into a subject index and a "Table of Statutes to Regulations." It is best to search in the subject index by topic rather than by agency name because entries for specific agencies lead primarily to regulations about the organization and procedures of that agency. Entries cite regulations by title and section number, with the title number first, followed by a colon, followed by the section number without a section symbol. The "Master Index" is issued once a year and is current through the final *Register* of the preceding year.

The OAL website provides a link to the electronic version of the CCR at http://ccr.oal.ca.gov that offers a number of ways to search for regulations. If you are looking for a specific section, you can type in the title and section number. Alternatively, you can use a standard word search, which will bring up a list of every regulation that contains those words. You can also click on a list of CCR titles and work your way through the table of contents for each title. Finally, you can click on the agency list, which will bring up the name and address of every agency with regulations in the CCR. Under the agency's name and address you will find a hyperlink to the location in the CCR of that agency's regulations, which may appear in more than one title.

Once you find a regulation in either source, read the text of the regulation carefully. Many techniques used for reading statutes apply

Figure 7-4. Example of a California Regulation

Title 19 Cal. Code Regs.

§ 986 Classification

(a) Fireworks or pyrotechnic devices that are to be used or sold for use in this state and found by the State Fire Marshal to come within the definition of "party poppers", "snap caps", "safe and sane", "agricultural and wildlife", "model rocket motors", "high power rocket motors", "emergency signaling device", or "exempt" fireworks shall be classified as such by the State Fire Marshal.

EXCEPTION: Special Effects Items Developed and Compounded on Location for Single Time Usage.

(b) The classification of an item shall not be construed as conferring classification to any similar item without the approval of the State Fire Marshal. The trade name of an item shall not be changed without notifying the State Fire Marshal 30 days prior to such change.

NOTE: Authority cited: Sections 12552 and 12553, Health and Safety Code. Reference: Sections 12560–12569 and 12671, Health and Safety Code.

HISTORY

1. Renumbering of article heading, amendment of section text and new NOTE filed 4-14-92; operative 5-14-92 (Register 92, No. 21).
2. Amendment of subsection (a) filed 6-24-94; operative 6-24-94 (Register 94, No. 25).

Source: *Barclays Official California Code of Regulations*, volume 21, page 67 (2008).

equally well to reading administrative regulations. For example, you should always look for a separate rule that provides definitions, be aware of cross-references, read the text several times, and outline any complicated provisions. Figure 7-4 provides an example of a California regulation concerning fireworks.

Following the text of each regulation you will see a "Note" that includes an authority citation to the statute that enables the agency to adopt regulations and a reference citation that indicates the statutes that this regulation implements, interprets, or makes specific. After these citations you will see a "History" section, which is provided whenever a regulation is adopted, amended, repealed, renumbered, or includes an editorial correction. Since the legal issue you are researching will be controlled by the regulation in effect when the issue arose, you need to read the history note to learn of any changes to the rule since that time.

D. *California Regulatory Notice Register*

Just as legislatures enact statutes throughout a year, agencies take regulatory actions daily. To inform the public of these actions, the OAL publishes the *California Regulatory Notice Register* weekly. It is commonly referred to as the "Z Register." The Z Register serves several functions. First, it is the location where agencies are required by the APA to publish all proposed actions on regulations. These notices may include an "informative digest/policy overview" discussing the nature of the proposed regulation, a prediction of the likely cost to local agencies, a consideration of reasonable alternatives, and the effect on small business. The notices must include information on where the public can get the full text of the proposed regulation, when and where members of the public may submit comments, and the time and place of any public meeting. The Z Register also contains notices of general public interest, OAL determinations on alleged underground regulations, OAL decisions disapproving proposed regulatory changes, and a summary of regulations filed with the secretary of state. The Z Register is available both in print and on the OAL website.

Researching in the Z Register in print to find proposed regulatory action is difficult. There is no index or other finding tool for the Z Register. However, under the APA, agency action must be completed within one year of the date of the publication of the notice of proposed action. Therefore, a researcher needs to go through only 12 months of Z Registers following the first notice in order to be sure what happened to the proposed regulation. The issues for the year in which you are researching and for some of the preceding year may be available in your library. They are also available online on the OAL website in PDF format.

The Government Code requires that all agencies that intend to undertake regulatory activity in a calendar year must prepare a rulemaking calendar by January 30 of that year. The combined calendar for all agencies becomes available several months later.[13] You can use this calendar to learn what administrative actions are scheduled for the upcoming year, which will tell you if you need to keep track of notices in the Z Register that might affect regulations that might affect your client.

Another print source of information is *Barclays Digest of New Regulations*, which as discussed earlier is published along with the weekly *California Regulatory Code Supplement*. The *Digest* includes all amendments to regulations that the OAL has approved and filed with the secretary of state in a one-week period. The *Digest* is a useful source to check to see if a regulation you are researching has been changed in the recent past.

The most reliable source of information on pending regulatory action is the agency itself. You can contact agencies directly. In addition, agencies are increasingly setting up their own websites. Any agency that has a website is required by the APA to post information concerning its regulatory actions on the site.[14] If you need to keep track of pending regulations on a regular basis, members of the public and interested organizations can request a state agency to put them on a mailing list to be notified directly of any proposed regulatory actions.[15]

E. Agency Decisions

The Administrative Procedure Act not only controls administrative regulations and rulemaking, but also has provisions for agency adjudication.[16] Adjudications involve primarily decisions of those

---

13. The 2008 Rulemaking Calendar became available online and in print at the end of March, 2008. Source: www.oal.ca.gov/rulemaking _intro.htm.

14. Cal. Govt. Code Ann. § 11340.85(c) (Lexis Supp. 2008).

15. Cal. Govt. Code Ann. § 11346.4(a)(1) (Lexis Supp. 2008).

16. Cal. Govt. Code Ann. §§ 11370–11528 (Lexis 1997 & Supp. 2008).

agencies that issue professional or occupational licenses and administer entitlement benefits, as well as personnel decisions of many agencies. Some of these adjudications occur through mediation or arbitration; these proceedings and their results are confidential. Other adjudications involve some kind of hearing process presided over by an administrative law judge (ALJ); these decisions become public record. California law authorizes both informal and formal hearings. Some larger agencies have their own ALJs, but others use a centralized pool of independent ALJs provided by the Office of Administrative Hearings.

Agency decisions must be written, must be based on the record, and must include a statement of both the factual and the legal basis for the decision.[17] Since 1997, adjudicative decisions by agencies may be designated as precedential; barring such a designation, an agency may not rely on a previous decision as precedent.[18] Agencies must keep an index of "significant legal and policy determinations made in precedent decisions," and the index must be available to the public by subscription.[19]

Despite the requirements that adjudicatory decisions must be written and agencies must keep an index of precedential decisions, finding such decisions is difficult. No method of printing, indexing, or digesting has been created. Some can be found on either LexisNexis or Westlaw. Agencies that have websites and issue decisions include precedential decisions and perhaps non-precedential decisions on their websites. A researcher has to know which agency's website to search and may have to look around the website carefully to find the decisions. Agencies will respond to direct requests, but researchers generally need both a case name and a case number to get a useful answer.

Administrative orders may be appealed to a California Superior Court for review. California courts have jurisdiction to review the va-

---

17. Cal. Govt. Code Ann. §§ 11425.10(a)(6), 11425.50 (Lexis 1997).
18. Cal. Govt. Code Ann. §§ 11425.10(a)(7), 11425.60(a) (Lexis 1997).
19. Cal. Govt. Code Ann. § 11425.60(c) (Lexis 1997).

lidity of both regulations and agency adjudications.[20] Conducting case research may reveal cases that address the agency rules and orders relevant to your research.

F. Attorney General Opinions

The attorney general is the state's lawyer. In that role, the attorney general provides opinions that are similar to the advice of an attorney to a client. A formal opinion from the attorney general responds to a specific question posed by a state or local public officer. The California Constitution and statutes restrict those who can ask for a formal opinion from the attorney general to constitutional officers, legislators, state agencies, state boards or commissions, district attorneys, county counsels, sheriffs, city prosecutors, and judges.

Even though attorney general opinions come from a branch of the government, they are not primary authority because they are considered advisory only. Courts may, however, find them persuasive if there is no relevant primary authority, and in that instance they are "entitled to great weight."[21] An opinion of the attorney general that has stood for a significant period of time is highly persuasive because courts assume that the legislature was aware of the opinion and could have changed or clarified the law had it disagreed.[22]

Opinions are numbered as they are assigned to be drafted, with a six-digit number that indicates the year and month assigned, and the order in which the opinion was assigned. For example, the opinion

---

20. Cal. Govt. Code Ann. § 11350 authorizes declaratory judgments as to the validity of regulations; Cal. Govt. Code Ann. § 11460 authorizes declaratory judgments as to the results of infomal agency hearings; Cal. Govt. Code Ann. § 11523 authorizes review of the results of formal agency hearings through a writ of mandate.

21. *Phyle v. Duffy*, 334 U.S. 431, 441 (1948).

22. *Napa Valley Educators' Assn. v. Napa Valley Unified Sch. Dist.*, 194 Cal. App. 3d 243, 251 (1st Dist. 1987).

responding to the question, "May a redevelopment agency discuss proposed terms of a lease agreement in a closed session?" was assigned the number 07-1202 indicating that it was assigned in 2007 and was the second opinion assigned in December.

California attorney general opinions have been published since 1943 in *Opinions of the Attorney General of California.* There is a volume for each year. Once an opinion is published, it is given a citation consisting of the volume and page number. Each volume contains the text of opinions published in that year, a numerical table of opinions, a table of opinions cited, a table of statutes, and a subject index. Because of these indexes, finding a relevant attorney general opinion in print is relatively straightforward. Separate indexes were published for the period 1943–1972 and 1973–1982. Since 1983, each volume of *Opinions of the Attorney General of California* includes a cumulative index, with a ten-year cumulative index being included at appropriate intervals. Therefore, the volume for 1992 includes the ten-year index and tables for 1983–1992, and the volume for 2002 includes the ten-year index and tables for 1993–2002. The indexes and tables in the most recently published volume for 2007 include references to opinions from 2002 through 2007, and the 2012 volume should include a ten-year cumulative index for 2003–2012.

Attorney general opinions published since 1986 can be researched online at http://ag.ca.gov/opinions. You can perform a search using words, phrases, or the number of a specific opinion. You can also look through the yearly index from 1997 forward, which includes a short summary of each opinion. Finally, there is a Monthly Opinion Report on the site that lists pending assignments and provides links to newly issued opinions.

IV. Federal Administrative Law

The federal government's agencies function much like California's. Agencies such as the Securities and Exchange Commission, the National Labor Relations Board, and the Bureau of Reclamation administer the laws enacted by Congress, promulgate regulations that act like statutes, and adjudicate disputes in judicial proceedings.

The federal APA is codified at 5 U.S.C. § 551 et seq. Its goal is to promote uniformity, public participation, and public confidence in the fairness of the procedures used by agencies of the federal government.

A. *Code of Federal Regulations*

As in California, federal administrative rules are called "regulations." Federal regulations are published in the *Code of Federal Regulations* (C.F.R.), which is published by the Government Printing Office (GPO). C.F.R. is a codification of regulations issued by all federal agencies. C.F.R. is organized into fifty titles according to agency and subject. Unfortunately, the subjects of the C.F.R. titles do not all correspond to the subjects of the titles of the United States Code. For example, Title 29 in both U.S.C. and C.F.R. pertains to labor law, but Title 16 of U.S.C. pertains to Conservation, while Title 16 of C.F.R. addresses Commercial Practices. (See Figure 7-5 for an example of a federal regulation concerning fireworks.)

C.F.R. volumes are updated annually,[23] with about one-fourth of them updated each quarter. Titles 1 through 16 are updated as of January 1; Titles 17 through 27 are updated as of April 1; Titles 28 through 41 are updated as of July 1; and Titles 42 through 50 are updated as of October 1. Because of the vagaries of the GPO, however, updates may not be in your library until months after the schedule indicates. C.F.R. is a softbound series whose spines and part of the cover are in color. Each year, the GPO changes the color of the volumes as it prints the new volumes. The color change makes it easy to know if any particular volume is this year's or last year's. If no changes were made in a particular volume for the new year, a cover with the new color is pasted on the old volume.

To research a topic in C.F.R., you may use the general index. Look up your research terms or the relevant agency's name, and then read

---

23. The exception is Title 3, "The President," which includes executive orders. Unlike other C.F.R. titles, it is not updated annually.

Figure 7-5. Example of a Federal Regulation

16 C.F.R. § 1507.3 Fuses

TITLE 16 - COMMERCIAL PRACTICES

CHAPTER II - CONSUMER PRODUCT SAFETY COMMISSION

PART 1507 - FIREWORKS DEVICES

Sec. 1507.3 Fuses

(a) Fireworks devices that require a fuse shall:

(1) Utilize only a fuse that has been treated or coated in such manner as to reduce the possibility of side ignition. Devices such as ground spinners that require a restricted orifice for proper thrust and contain less than 6 grams of pyrotechnic composition are exempted from § 1507.3(a)(1).

(2) Utilize only a fuse which will burn at least 3 seconds but not more than 9 seconds before ignition of the device.

(b) The fuse shall be securely attached so that it will support either the weight of the fireworks plus 8 ounces of dead weight or double the weight of the device, whether [sic] is less, without separation from the fireworks device.

Source: *Code of Federal Regulations*, Title 16, Part 1000 to End, pages 539–540 (2008).

the referenced regulations. An easier way to find relevant regulations may be to begin your research in either *United States Code Annotated*, either in print or on Westlaw, or *United States Code Service*, either in print or on LexisNexis. Both annotated codes include references to related regulations for each statutory section if regulations exist. After finding a statute on point, review the annotations following the statutory language for cross-references to regulations. You may notice that *United States Code Service* tends to provide more references to regulations than does *United States Code Annotated*. In paper, look up the citations given; online, simply use the hyperlink to go directly to the regulation.

Federal regulations are available on LexisNexis and Westlaw. They are also available online at GPO Access, at www.gpoaccess.gov/cfr. The text there is no more current than the print versions, but those skilled in online research may prefer this site. The site allows searching by keyword, citation, and title. Like all other government web-sites, the GPO Access site is free of charge. Other free online sources—such as the website of the Center for Regulatory Effectiveness (www.thecre.com) and some law libraries—also provide access to C.F.R., but they do so by connecting with the GPO Access site. Finally, the subscription service HeinOnline (www.heinonline.org) also has a full database of C.F.R. in PDF files; if your library subscribes to HeinOnline, you may be able to access C.F.R. through that site.

B. *Federal Register*

New regulations and proposed changes to existing regulations are published first in the *Federal Register*, the federal equivalent of the weekly *California Regulatory Notice Register* (the "Z Register"). The *Federal Register* publishes all notices of proposed rulemaking, including notices of proposed amendments to existing rules, notices of hearings, responses to public comments on proposed regulations, and helpful tables and indexes. Unlike California's Z Register, the *Federal Register* includes the full text of both proposed and final regulations. The *Federal Register* is the first print source to publish regulations in their final form when they are adopted (i.e., before they are codified in C.F.R.). The *Federal Register* is published almost every weekday, with continuous pagination throughout the year. Each volume of the *Federal Register* covers a single calendar year, and page numbers reach the tens of thousands in the last few months of the year. The online version of the *Federal Register* is available through www.gpoaccess.gov; the site covers the years 1994 to the present. Both LexisNexis and Westlaw include the *Federal Register*; LexisNexis's coverage begins on July 1, 1980, and Westlaw's coverage begins on January 2, 1981. The *Federal Register* can also be found through the subscription service HeinOnline; this service's coverage begins with volume 1 in 1936 and currently extends through November, 2007.

C. Updating Federal Regulations

To update a federal regulation in print or on the government's website, begin with a small booklet or the database called *List of CFR Sections Affected* (LSA). As its name suggests, LSA lists all sections of C.F.R. that have been affected by recent agency action. LSA provides page references to *Federal Register* issues where action affecting a section of C.F.R. is included. If the section you are researching is not listed in LSA, it has not been changed since the C.F.R. was last revised. LSA is published monthly and is available online at www.gpoaccess.gov/lsa.

Final updating in print and on the web requires reference to a table at the back of the *Federal Register* called "CFR Parts Affected During [the current month]." (Do not confuse this table with the "CFR Parts Affected in this [Current] Issue" located in the Contents at the beginning of each issue.) Refer to this table in each *Federal Register* for the last day of each month for all of the months between the most recent LSA issue and the current date. Also check the most recent issue of *Federal Register* for the present month. The table contains relatively general information (whether a "part" has been affected, not a "section"), but will note changes made since the most recent LSA. Online CFR Parts Affected is available at www.gpoaccess.gov/lsa/curlist.html.

Both LexisNexis and Westlaw provide versions of C.F.R. that are updated to within two weeks of the date on which you look at them.

D. Decisions of Federal Agencies

Like some California agencies, some federal agencies hold quasi-judicial hearings to decide cases that arise under the agencies' regulations or jurisdiction. Some of these decisions are published in reporters specific to each agency, for example, *Decisions and Orders of the National Labor Relations Board*. A comprehensive list of federal agency reporters is available through the website of Washburn University School of Law at http://washlaw.edu/doclaw/executive5m.html.

E. Judicial Opinions

The methods of case research explained in Chapter 3 will lead to opinions in which the judiciary reviewed decision of federal agencies. Additionally, C.F.R. can be updated to find relevant cases using *Shepard's Code of Federal Regulations Citations*, both in print and online on LexisNexis, or Westlaw's KeyCite. These citators are addressed in Chapter 8.

.

Chapter 8

Updating Legal Authority

Ensuring that the authorities found during legal research represent the *current* law is a critical step in the research process. A few examples demonstrate why: a case decided in 1990 may have subsequently been overruled, a case decided last year may have been reversed on appeal, and a recently enacted statute may have just been declared unconstitutional. These three authorities would still appear in print and online sources, but they may not be relied on in legal analysis. Determining whether an authority is current and respected is called *updating*; this step is sometimes referred to as "Shepardizing" because the first major updating tool was a print series called *Shepard's Citations*.

Updating an authority requires examining each legal source that has subsequently cited that authority and determining how the subsequent source treated your authority on a particular issue. A *citator* provides a list of citations to those sources that refer to your authority. Online citators provide the most comprehensive and up-to-date lists, so they are the focus of this chapter.[1] Citators are also valuable tools for expanding research. By reading cases that have cited a relevant authority, you will quickly find other authorities on the same topic.

I. Online Citators

The two leading online providers of legal material both have extensive citator services. "Shepard's" is the online citator available on

---

1. An appendix at the end of the chapter briefly covers the use of print citators.

133

Table 8-1. Outline for Updating Online

1. Access the citator and enter the citation of the cited source in the box provided.
2. Select the type of citation list needed:
   - a short list for validating the cited source (to examine any negative treatment by later cases), or
   - an extensive list of all citing sources.
3. Evaluate the analytical symbols provided by the citator.
4. Limit the citator results by jurisdiction, headnote, date, or other function.
5. Prioritize and read the citing sources. Analyze the impact, if any, these sources have on the cited source.

LexisNexis; Westlaw provides a competing service called "KeyCite." Their coverage of California material is not identical, though both cover cases, statutes, constitutional provisions, administrative regulations, and some secondary sources.[2]

The process of updating online is summarized in Table 8-1. Understanding that process requires familiarity with two basic terms: the *cited source* and the *citing sources*. The authority you are updating, in the following example a California case,[3] is called the *cited source*. The authorities listed in a citator that refer to that case are called *citing*

---

2. The "Scope" link provides updated information about KeyCite coverage. The "Scope" link is located toward the bottom of the main KeyCite webpage. Shepard's provides a "Product Guide" that is available from the Shepard's tab by clicking the "Help" link.

3. While this chapter uses a case to illustrate the updating process, KeyCite and Shepard's cover statutes, constitutions, federal and California administrative regulations, law review articles, restatements, and many other legal authorities.

sources or sometimes *citing references*. For each updating search there is only one cited source while there may be many citing sources.

Both KeyCite and Shepard's include color-coded symbols that provide a quick reference to researchers indicating whether a particular authority is still good law. These symbols are listed in Tables 8-4 and 8-5 later in this chapter. While these symbols are helpful, they do not merit too much weight. A red symbol may mean that only a portion of the case was overruled; you can still rely on such a case for a different point of law. Similarly, do not take too much comfort when no red symbol appears. Be sure to read the citing references and decide for yourself whether your case is still "good law."

II. Updating Cases

A. KeyCite on Westlaw

1. Access the Citator

KeyCite can be accessed on Westlaw in three different ways:

- through a KeyCite link at the top of the search screen,
- by typing a citation into the KeyCite box in the left frame, and
- from any source that displays a KeyCite symbol (by clicking on that symbol).

This chapter begins with the KeyCite link because it provides essential information, including an overview of analysis symbols used, a list of publications that can be updated using KeyCite, and tips on a number of KeyCite topics.

The KeyCite link connects to a page that is divided into left and right frames. The right frame explains the symbols used to show links between the citing references and the case being updated. Table 8-4, which appears later in this chapter, summarizes some of the symbols used for cases in KeyCite.

In the left frame is a box for typing in the citation. To learn the citation format used by KeyCite, or whether a particular publication is included in KeyCite, click on the "Publications List" link in the left frame.

2. Select the Type of Citing List

The default citation list for KeyCite is called "Full History," indicated by an arrow next to "Full History" in the left frame. (See Figure 8-2.) Despite its name, this list contains only the direct history and negative treatment of the cited source, not a full list of citing references. The first sources listed under Full History show the litigation process of the cited case, i.e., the direct history of the case.[4] This list of sources shows, for example, whether the case was affirmed on appeal or whether it reversed and remanded a lower court decision. Next in Full History, KeyCite lists "Negative Citing References." These are sources that KeyCite has identified as providing important negative treatment of your case.

With limited time to update a case, at least skim the sources appearing under Full History. To pull up a separate window showing the actual text of a source listed, click on the number immediately preceding that source's entry in the citation list. Similarly, to pull up the KeyCite page of a citing source, click on the treatment symbol (e.g., a red flag or a green "C") preceding that source's entry in the list.

The more comprehensive list of citing sources is called "Citing References," as shown in Figure 8-3. It is accessed by clicking on "Citing References" in the left frame. The Citing References page first lists those sources that have treated the cited case negatively, then those that provide positive treatment. Within each category, sources are organized according to green "Depth of Treatment" stars. Four stars indicate a citing reference provides an extensive discussion of the cited source. As the length of the discussion of the cited source decreases, the number of stars is reduced. Three stars indicate a less-extensive discussion of the cited source, while two stars indicate little discussion. One star

---

4. "Direct History (Graphical View)" provides that information in flow-chart format.

Figure 8-2. Full History on KeyCite

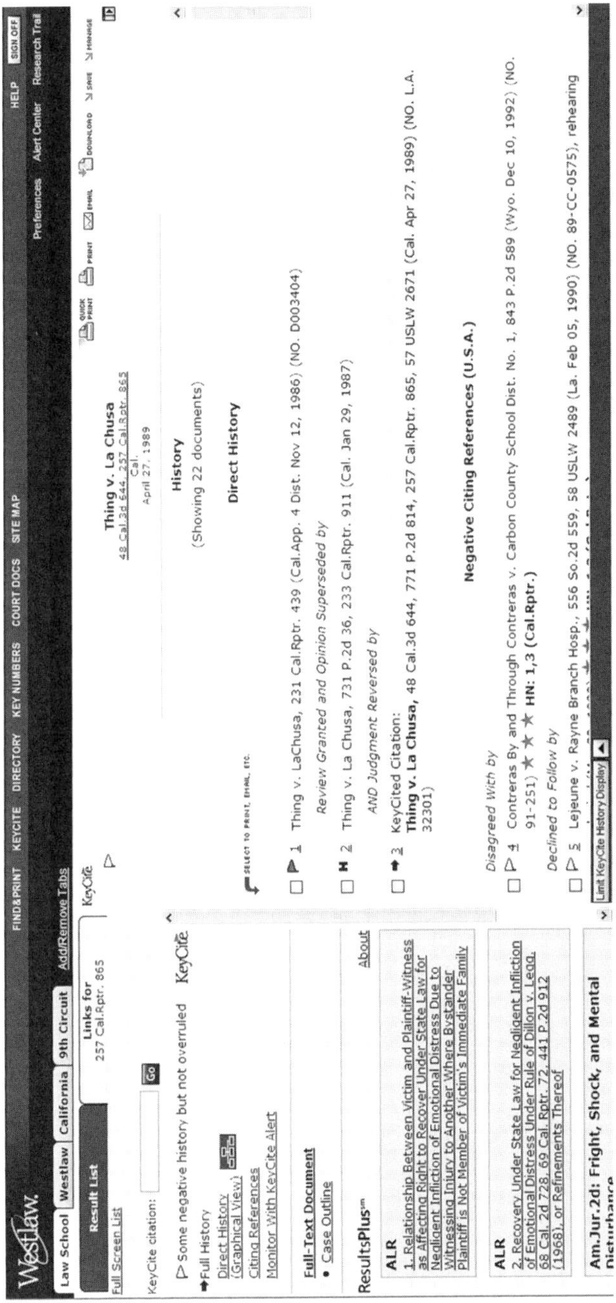

Source: Westlaw. Reprinted with permission of West, a Thomson business.

Figure 8-3. Citing References on KeyCite

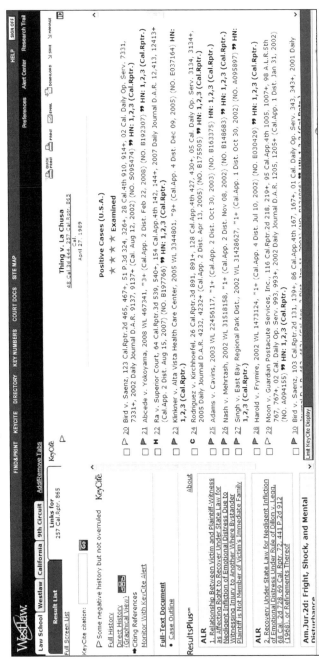

Source: Westlaw (showing the first positive treatment cases, in a list of over 1,500 total citing references). Reprinted with permission of West, a Thomson business.

Table 8-4. Selected Symbols for Updating Cases with KeyCite

KeyCite Symbol	Meaning
Red flag	Negative treatment; the case is no longer good law for at least one point, e.g., at least a portion of the case has been reversed or overruled
Yellow flag	Some negative treatment, but the case has not been reversed or overruled
Blue "H"	Direct history for the case is available, and it is not known to be negative (note that these cases may have citing references, although that is not clear from KeyCite's current explanations)
Green "C"	No direct history for the case is available; the case has citing references and they are not known to be negative

means that the cited source is merely mentioned by the citing reference, perhaps in a string cite. Within star categories, citing references are organized by jurisdiction, court, and date of decision. A source that quotes the cited source is noted with purple quotation marks.

3. Analyze the Citator Symbols

KeyCite has assigned a quick-reference symbol to each authority that can be updated. The symbol is given both in the left frame and at the top-left of the right frame. A summary of some of these symbols is provided in Table 8-4. These symbols are only preliminary indicators of whether a case is still "good law"; you must read citing sources that seem to bear on your issue and determine for yourself the continued validity of the cited source.

The same symbols also precede each citing source. These symbols show the KeyCite assessment of the strength of each citing source, as opposed to that of the cited case. If a citing source has a negative symbol, its impact on the cited case may be minimal; since other sources disagree with that source, its overall authoritative value is decreased.

4. Limit the Search Results

Some authorities have been cited by many sources, and reading all of them is often unrealistic. For example, the *Thing* case shown in Figure 8-3 has over 1,500 citing references. To concentrate on the citing sources that appear most relevant to your project, click on the "Limit KeyCite Display" button in the bottom-left of the right KeyCite frame. This will bring up a "KeyCite Limits" page. The categories of available restrictions are listed in the left frame of this page. The citator list for *Thing* can be restricted by headnotes, locate (e.g., keyword search), jurisdiction, date, document type (e.g., cases, secondary sources, court documents), and depth of treatment. Click on a category to see its restrictions in the right frame of the page. Specify all desired restrictions and then click the "Apply" button in the left frame to see the filtered search results.

5. Read and Analyze the Citing Sources

While KeyCite can alert you to possible problems through colored flags and treatment stars, only you can decide the impact of an authority on the case you want to use in your analysis. Thus, the most important aspect of updating is reading and analyzing the history cases and citing references.

With an online citator, accessing these references is easy. Click on an authority in the KeyCite list to view the point in the corresponding document where your case is cited. Quickly skim that portion of the document and decide whether the source is relevant to your research. If it is, read the citing source carefully and analyze its impact on the cited case: Does the citing source change the rule of law in the cited case, perhaps by reversing or overruling it? Does it follow the cited case by simply restating the rule and applying it to a similar fact pattern? Does the new source distinguish or criticize the cited case? If so, why and how?

Sometimes a citing source does not address the legal question at issue in your research project. If a source analyzes only points of the cited case that are not relevant to your project, disregard that source.

Reading and analyzing the citing sources provides research benefits beyond determining whether the cited case is still "good law." A citing source may have facts more similar to your client's situation. A court may make a point in a particularly helpful way. Or a citing source may raise a related claim that you had not previously considered. To take advantage of these benefits, and to avoid relying on quick-reference symbols to decide whether a case is still valid, include ample time in the research process for updating.

B. Shepard's on LexisNexis

1. Access the Citator

Shepard's can be accessed from two points on LexisNexis.

- Click on the "Shepardize" link at the top of a document displayed on your screen.
- Click on the "Shepard's" tab from any screen and type the citation of the cited source into the box. For help with the format used by Shepard's, click on the "Citation Formats" link to the right of the box.

2. Select the Type of Citing List

Select the appropriate button for the desired list of citing sources. "Shepard's for Validation" provides a limited list of citing sources, intended only to show whether the case is still good law. This short list is similar to KeyCite's "Full History" list. "Shepard's for Validation" limits results to subsequent appellate history, citing references with editorial analysis, and citing references that have been added in the past two months. With limited time for updating, at least consider each case that appears in "Shepard's for Validation."

To obtain a complete list of citing sources, click on "Shepard's for Research," which is analogous to KeyCite's list of "Citing References." At the top of the page, Shepard's provides a summary of how many citing sources were found and provides a breakdown of how those sources treated the cited source. By clicking on each category listed in the summary, you can view all of the authorities that treated the cited source in a particular way, such as "followed." When viewing the entire list of results from "Shepard's for Research," a case's "prior history" will be given first, followed by citing references arranged by hierarchy (highest courts first) and date (most recent cases first). Following case references, secondary citing sources such as law review articles are presented in alphabetical order.

3. Analyze the Citator Symbols

The top of the results page has a symbol that indicates the opinion of Shepard's attorney-editors regarding the validity of the cited source. To learn what a particular symbol means, rest your mouse pointer over the symbol. For a full list of symbols and their meanings, click on the "Legend" link in the bottom-left corner of the screen. Alternatively, scroll down to the abbreviated legend provided at the bottom of any Shepard's results screen. A list of symbols is provided in Table 8-5.

Each Shepard's results screen on LexisNexis begins with a summary of results, typically in a grey box. This summary shows the number of times the cited source has been followed, distinguished, criticized, explained, etc. Clicking on one of these terms will allow you to skip through the search results to each citing source that treats your case in that way. To go to the cases that distinguish your au-

Table 8-5. Symbols for Updating Cases with Shepard's

Shepard's Symbol	Meaning
Red stop sign	Negative treatment; the case may no longer be good law, e.g., the case has been reversed or overruled
Orange "Q"	Treatment questions the case's continuing validity or precedential value
Yellow triangle	Possible negative treatment, e.g., the case has been limited or criticized
Blue "A"	Citing sources are available, but they are neither positive nor negative, e.g., an appeal or writ of certiorari has been denied
Blue "I"	Citing sources are available, but they do not have treatment symbols, e.g., another case or a law review article merely cites the case
Green diamond	Positive treatment, e.g., the case has been affirmed or followed

thority, for example, click on "Distinguished" in the summary box.[5] The summary also includes the number of non-case citing sources, such as law review articles, and the number of times each LexisNexis headnote in the case has been referenced. Figure 8-6 shows the first screen of the case *Thing v. La Chusa*, using Shepard's for Research.

Each citing source is shown with its own Shepard's symbol at the end of the source's citation in the Shepard's results list, as shown in Figures 8-6 and 8-7. As with KeyCite, it is important not to confuse these symbols with the symbol for the case you are updating. The more useful symbol is the one at the top of the page that gives the Shepard's view of your case. Clicking a symbol next to a citing source will display the Shepard's for Research list for that source. Clicking

---

5. Some browsers do not support this function. An alternative is to use the "Find" function on your computer.

Figure 8-6. Shepard's for Research

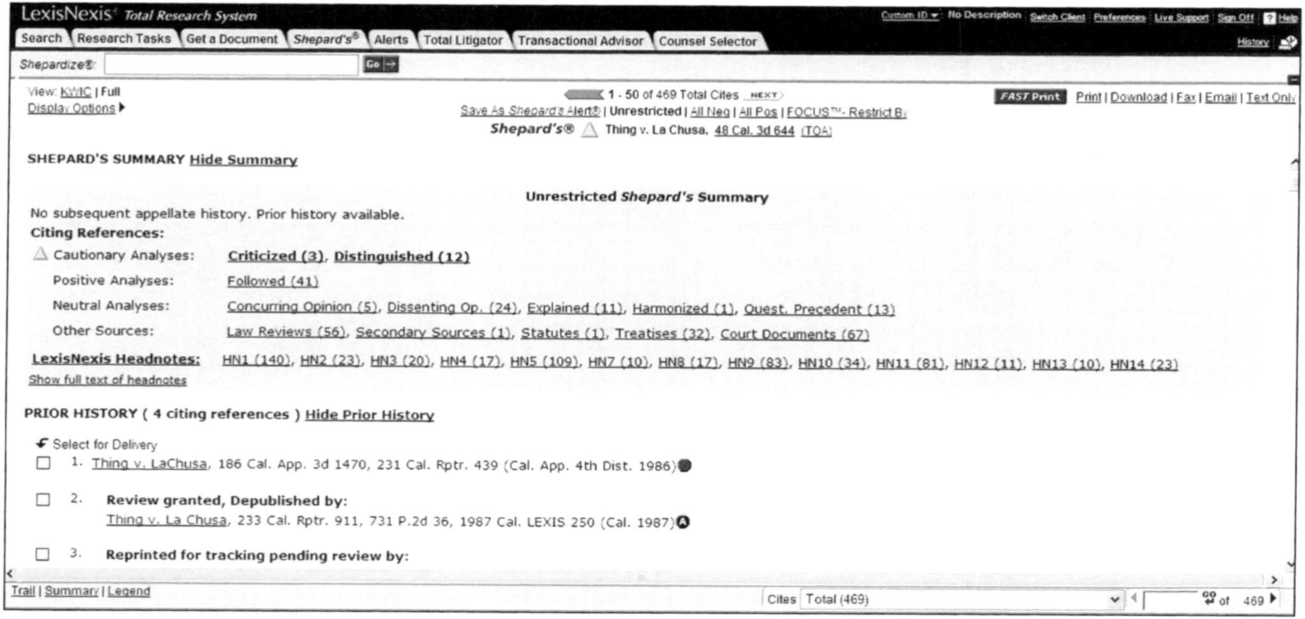

Source: LexisNexis. LexisNexis and the Knowledge Burst Logo are registered trademarks of Reed Elsevier Properties Inc., used with the permission of LexisNexis.

Figure 8-7. Shepard's Citing Sources

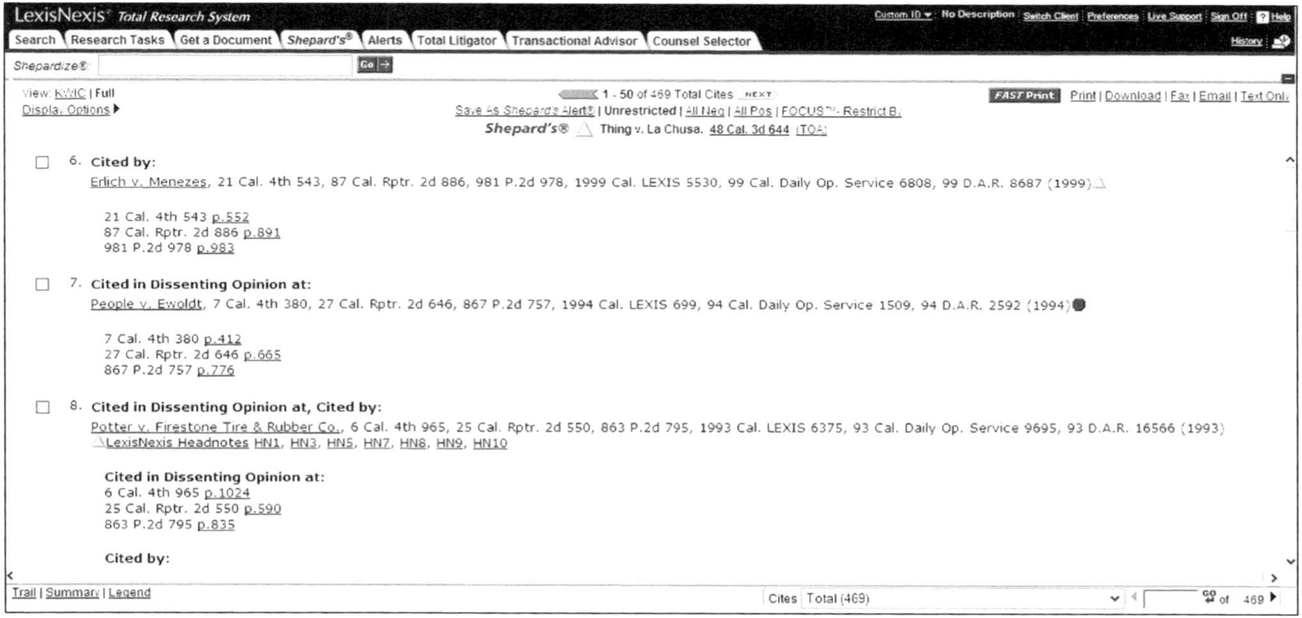

Source: LexisNexis. LexisNexis and the Knowledge Burst Logo are registered trademarks of Reed Elsevier Properties Inc., used with the permission of LexisNexis.

on the name of the source will take you either to the first page of that source or the portions that refer to the cited source.

4. Limit the Search Results

Results can be sorted into lists of positive authority ("All Pos") and negative authority ("All Neg") using links at the top of the Shepard's page. As with KeyCite, the search results can also be filtered. This feature in Shepard's is called "FOCUS—Restrict By" and is provided via a link at the top of any Shepard's page. Following that link for the *Thing* case, you would see a screen where you could filter by analysis (e.g., the treatment the citing sources gave *Thing*), key words (called "FOCUS Terms"), jurisdiction, the type of authority (e.g., case, statute, secondary source, etc.), the points of law in the LexisNexis headnotes of the cited case that the citing sources address, and date. Simply click on the desired options (leave the rest blank) and click the "Apply" button at the bottom of the page. The filtered list of Shepard's results will be displayed.

5. Read and Analyze the Citing Sources

Again, the most important aspect of updating is reading the citing sources and deciding the impact they have on the cited source. As noted above, clicking on the pinpoint link for a citing source will take you to the point in that source's text where your case is cited, making it easy to determine whether the source is relevant to your research.

C. Prioritizing Citing Sources

When time allows, you should read *every* citing source to determine its impact on the case you are updating and to see whether it adds to your analysis. When pressed for time, however, prioritize the citing sources you will read according to the following criteria:

- *Negative treatment.* Look for any case that reverses, overrules, criticizes, or distinguishes your case.
- *Jurisdiction.* Read cases from your jurisdiction before reading cases decided elsewhere, which are only persuasive authority.
- *Hierarchy.* Read cases from the highest appellate court, then the intermediate appellate courts, and finally the trial courts (if trial court cases are published) in your jurisdiction.
- *Date.* Start with more recent cases rather than older cases.
- *Headnotes.* Prioritize citing sources that refer to the headnotes from the cited case that are on point for your research.

Sorting documents online by headnote reference requires close attention to the various sources that may publish a case. A single case may have been published in multiple reporters or online databases, and thus may have three sets of headnotes: one set in the official reporter, a second set in a West reporter (and on Westlaw), and a third set in a Lexis Publishing reporter (and on LexisNexis). Each source may have a different number of headnotes, and the substance of each headnote may be different. If you are interested in a particular headnote from a West reporter and accordingly filter Shepard's results by that headnote number, your results will be useless.

Even when working within a single company's resources (e.g., using Shepard's to update a case you read on LexisNexis), remember that headnote notations given in a citator list refer to the relevant headnote in the cited case. The same point of law will probably be discussed in a headnote with a different number in the various citing sources. This is because, while headnotes in the cited source and the citing sources may address the same point of law, they may not match up number for number.

III. Updating Statutes

The basic process of updating statutes with KeyCite and LexisNexis is the same as the process of updating cases: enter a citation on the appropriate screen, review the sources listed, examine the symbols (if any), restrict the search, and read the citing sources.

As with cases, both services provide two lists. On KeyCite, "History" provides legislative background, including reports of the legislature and the derivation of the statute. "Citing References" provides links to cases and other sources that have cited the statute. On LexisNexis, Shepard's provides a short list under "Shepard's for Validation" and a more comprehensive list under "Shepard's for Research."

Both services provide colored symbols that suggest the validity of the statute; obviously the precise meaning of each symbol is different from when the symbol refers to cases. For example, on KeyCite a red flag for a statute may mean that the statute has been amended, repealed, superseded, held unconstitutional, or preempted. LexisNexis includes a unique symbol for statutes, an exclamation point noting negative case treatment.

When updating a statute online, begin with a citation to the smallest portion of the statute that is applicable to your research. For example, in updating the arson statute, Cal. Penal Code § 451, you could update just section (a) instead of updating the entire statute; the more restrictive search currently produces about half as many results. If you want the legislative history of a statute, however, you may need to enter the code number without subdivisions (e.g., just 451). As with any updating work, the most important step is to read the citing sources to determine how they treat the statute that you are updating.

IV. Updating Other Authorities

Many authorities from both federal and state jurisdictions can be updated online, including statutes, regulations, administrative materials, patents, and secondary sources. Both KeyCite and Shepard's are expanding their coverage, so check frequently for current information.

Appendix. Shepardizing in Print

The process of updating with *Shepard's Citators* in print is similar to updating online with one important exception: the citing references are contained in multiple volumes rather than in a comprehensive list. Table 8-A provides an outline for Shepardizing in print.

Table 8-A. Outline for Shepardizing in Print

1. Find the *Shepard's* series for the source you want to update.
2. Review the cover of the most recent *Shepard's* pamphlet for a chart called "What Your Library Should Contain." Gather the relevant *Shepard's* volumes and supplements listed in that chart.
3. Compile lists of citing references.
4. Analyze the citations and *Shepard's* analytical symbols.
5. Prioritize and read the citing sources. Analyze the impact, if any, these sources have on the cited source.

1. Select a **Shepard's** Series

Either the jurisdiction or the reporter where the cited case was published will indicate which *Shepard's* series you can use for updating. Lists of citations to California cases may be included in *Shepard's California Citations*[6] and *Shepard's Pacific Reporter Citations*. Shepardizing a California case in the two citator series may produce slightly different results since their coverage is slightly different. Tables at the front of each *Shepard's* volume state which citing sources are included.

---

6. This series includes cases from *California Reports*, *California Appellate Reports*, *Pacific Reporter*, and *California Reporter*. Be sure to consult the volumes in the series that include cases from the reporter that you are using.

2. Collect Relevant Shepard's Volumes

Each *Shepard's* series consists of several hardbound volumes and softbound supplements. Because *Shepard's* volumes and supplements are not cumulative, developing a comprehensive list of citing sources requires reference to all the volumes and pamphlets that cover the time span from when a case was decided to the present. On the cover of the most recent supplement[7] is a list called "What Your Library Should Contain." Review that list and collect the relevant volumes and supplements. *Shepard's* hardbound maroon volumes and supplements contain the most information, but they are soon outdated. These hardbound volumes are updated with softbound pamphlets with gold, red, white, or blue paper covers. The color indicates the period covered. Gold covers indicate annual or semi-annual updates. Red or blue covers indicate pamphlets with coverage over several months. White supplements, called *advance sheets*, generally cover just a few weeks.

The time spans covered by these different volumes and supplements do not overlap; thus, to compile a comprehensive list of citing sources, you may need to refer to multiple volumes and supplements. However, not every volume is necessary for every updating project. When updating a case, for example, volumes with statutes as cited sources are not needed. Also, volumes published before the date of your case are unnecessary because your case will not be included there.

3. Compile Lists of Citations from Multiple Shepard's Volumes

Look up your citation in each of the relevant volumes and supplements.[8] The example in Figure 8-B is for the case *People v. Davis*,

---

7. If a supplement is more than one month old, there is likely a more recent supplement available for use, although your library may not have received it yet. To determine whether a supplement is the most recent available, ask a librarian.

8. To begin without a citation but with one party's name, use *Shepard's Case Names Citator* or the Table of Cases in *California Digest 2d* to find the citation.

Figure 8-B. Excerpts from *Shepard's Pacific Reporter Citations* for *People v. Davis*, 958 P.2d 1083 (Cal. 1998)

– 1083 –	101CaR2d[1]282
People v. Davis	# 103CaR2d[1]
1998	[146
(18C4th712)	# 103CaR2d[2]
(76CaR2d 770)	[146
s 59CaR2d584	# 103CaR2d[3]
2007Cal LX	[147
[6758	120CaR2d134
46P3d923	120CaR2d[1]137
46P3d[1]925	f 120CaR2d139
f 46P3d926	d 120CaR2d[1]
d 46P3d[1]927	[140
d 46P3d928	d 120CaR2d141
47P3d293	120CaR2d513
86CaR2d[1]163	Mass
97CaR2d273	752NE2d772

Source: *Shepard's Pacific Reporter Citations*, 1994–2007 Bound Supplement, Case Edition, Part 4, page 883. Published by Lexis Publishing.

18 Cal. 4th 712, 958 P.2d 1083, 76 Cal. Rptr. 2d 770 (1998), in the bound supplement for 1994–2007 of *Shepard's Pacific Reporter Citations*. Similar entries exist in other volumes and supplements, although the *Davis* case will not be mentioned if no citing sources were published during the period of a particular volume or supplement.

4. Analyze the Citations and Shepard's Symbols

Any *parallel citations* will appear underneath the name of your case in the first *Shepard's* volume where your case appears. A parallel citation refers to an additional publication of the case in another reporter. Parallel citations will be enclosed in parentheses. The parallel cites for the *Davis* case are 18 Cal. 4th 712 and 76 Cal. Rptr. 2d 770.

After any parallel cites are all the citing sources, the authorities that cite your case. In the interest of space, *Shepard's* has devised its own abbreviation system. Refer to the table of abbreviations for various sources at the beginning of the Shepard's volumes.

The first citing sources listed are *history cases*. History cases indicate what happened to the case as it proceeded through the judicial system. All of these cases concern the same parties and facts in the same litigation. Just before each history citing source is a letter indicating how the citing source is related to the cited source. In the *Davis* example in Table 8-B, "s 59CaR2d584" refers to an earlier stage of this same litigation, the decision of the California Court of Appeal, Second District, to affirm the Superior Court's decision. Other history symbols include "a" for affirmed and "r" for reversed.

The next citing sources refer to the cited case, although they are unrelated to it. These cases involved different parties and different facts; in deciding these cases, the courts referred to your case. Each of these cases may be preceded by a *treatment* abbreviation, indicating how the citing source treated your case. Common treatment abbreviations are "o" for a later case that overruled the one you are updating, "f" for a source that followed that case you are updating, "e" for a source that explained your case, and "j" for a case that cited yours in a dissenting opinion. Keep in mind that, as in online updating, a treatment code might refer to a part of the case that is not relevant to your work. One abbreviation that is unique to California cases in *Shepard's* is the # symbol. This abbreviation signals that "the citing case is of questionable precedential value because review or rehearing has been granted by the California Supreme Court and/or the citing case has been ordered depublished pursuant to Rule 976 of the California Rules of Court. (Publication status should be verified before use of the citing case in California.)"

Note the difference between the page numbers given for history cases and for treatment cases. For history cases, because the citing case will be related to the parties and litigation of your case, the citation in the *Shepard's* list is to the *first page* of the citing case. For treatment cases, in contrast, your case will be mentioned on one, maybe two pages of the citing case. Therefore, for treatment cases, *Shepard's* lists the *specific page* where your case appears. This page number is analogous to pinpoint pages in a case citation. For example, in the

Davis citation list in the 1994–2007 bound volume, the entry "s 59CaR2d584" is a history source; the first page of that case is 584. The next entry for a published case[9] is "46P3d923," which refers to the case *People v. Valencia.* This is a treatment case; the *Davis* case is cited on page 923, though the first page of the *Valencia* case is 920. There are four additional entries for this case, each one on a different page because the *Valencia* court cited *Davis* more than once.

In print Shepardizing, the *headnote reference* does not appear at the end of the entry as it does online. Instead, it appears as a small superscript number located between the reporter abbreviation and the page number. For example, one of the *Valencia* entries reads: 46 P3d[1]925. The superscript number "1" between "3d" and "925" means that the point of law in headnote 1 of *Davis* is discussed on page 925 of *Valencia.* As with the online citators, you can use this superscript number as a finding tool to look specifically for cases that discuss the point of law in the cited case in which you are most interested, instead of skimming through many cases that turn out to discuss unrelated issues in the cited case.

Treatment cases are arranged by jurisdiction, beginning with the jurisdiction of the case being updated. Within that jurisdiction, cases are listed by court hierarchy and then in chronological order. Following cases, other sources that cite your case may be listed, such as law review articles.

5. Read and Analyze the Citing Sources

As in online updating, the most important step is to read and analyze the citing sources. While it is a good idea to read all of the citing sources, under time constraints you may choose to prioritize the sources you read, using the ideas listed earlier in this chapter.

---

9. *Shepard's* in print includes entries for cases that are available only online at the time the volume is printed. The entry immediately following the history source is "2007 LX 6758," a case then available only online. Since this print *Shepard's* volume was published, that California Supreme Court case has been published in all three available print reporters.

Chapter 9

Secondary Sources and Practice Aids

I. Introduction

Sources are deemed "secondary" when they are written by law professors, practicing attorneys, legal editors, or law students; in contrast, "primary" authority is written by legislatures, courts, and administrative agencies. Despite the terminology, secondary sources are invaluable in legal research, especially in research concerning an unfamiliar area of law. Remember that the research process outlined in Chapter 1 includes research in secondary sources as the second step.

Lawyers use secondary sources to learn about the law and to find references to relevant primary authority. Beginning a new research project—even in a familiar area of law—with a secondary source may be the most effective approach for three reasons. First, a secondary source may provide an overview of the pertinent issues, aiding in the analysis of the legal problem. Second, a secondary source will likely explain terminology and concepts, making it possible to develop a more effective list of research terms. Finally, secondary sources often provide a shortcut to researching primary authority by including numerous references to cases, statutes, and regulations.

This chapter introduces legal encyclopedias; treatises, practice guides, and other books; legal periodicals, including law reviews and bar journals; *American Law Reports*, a hybrid commentary-reporter; continuing legal education (CLE) publications; legal forms; topical

Table 9-1. Outline for Researching Secondary Sources in Print

---

1. Search the library's catalog for the titles and location of relevant secondary sources.
2. Search the index of a secondary source for research terms.
3. Find the relevant portion of the main volumes. Read the commentary to learn about the legal issues. Review footnotes or tables for references to primary authority.
4. Update the secondary source, if possible.

"mini-libraries"; restatements, uniform laws, and model codes; and jury instructions.[1] The chapter begins with a comparison of print and online research; it concludes with a discussion of when and how to use secondary sources in legal research.

II. Researching in Print or Online

Often researchers find that beginning a new project in print secondary sources is more effective than beginning in an online database. This preference especially holds true when researching a complicated issue in an unfamiliar area of law. Thus, this chapter concentrates on print sources. The process for researching secondary sources varies depending on the source. A general outline for researching secondary sources in print is provided in Table 9-1.

Many of the secondary sources discussed in this chapter can be found on LexisNexis, Westlaw, or other online services. The relevant databases can be searched by using terms-and-connectors searches or natural-language searches in the full text, and by reviewing tables of contents. In the early phases of research in a new area, searching the

---

1. Although the focus of this chapter is secondary sources, some primary authority is necessarily included. *American Law Reports* volumes include both articles and the full text of judicial opinions. Mini-libraries are valuable exactly because they combine in one place statutes, regulations, annotations to judicial and administrative decisions, and commentary.

Table 9-2. Selected Websites for California Research

Website	Address	Secondary Sources and Links
California State Bar	www.calbar.ca.gov	*California Bar Journal* CLE materials Bar forms Legal research links
Judicial Council Forms	www.courtinfo.ca.gov /forms	Mandatory and optional forms
Northern California Association of Law Libraries	www.nocall.org	Links to websites by legal topic
Witkin Legal Institute	www.witkin.com	Witkin products Current legal developments
The Recorder (formerly Cal Law)	www.law.com/jsp/ca	Legal news

online table of contents is more likely to be effective than other on-line searches. As you gain background knowledge in an area of law, full-text searches may become more effective.

Some secondary sources are available for free on state websites. A list of helpful websites for California research is provided in Table 9-2. In addition, a quick search on Google or other search engines may produce valuable leads. A law firm may refer to key statutes on its website, or an attorney may have posted a helpful summary of a legal issue. Before relying on these sources, consider the questions raised in Part XIII of this chapter.

III. Legal Encyclopedias

Like other encyclopedias, legal encyclopedias provide general in-formation on a wide variety of legal subjects. Legal encyclopedias are organized by subject matter under *topics*, which are presented alpha-betically in bound volumes. California has two encyclopedias: B.E.

Figure 9-3. Excerpt from Witkin on "Contracts"

[§ 179] Binding Purchase Agreement.

Whether an instrument creates an option or a contract of sale is determined not by its title or form, but by an analysis of the obligations imposed. (*Scarbery v. Bill Patch Land & Water Co.* (1960) 184 C.A.2d 87, 100, 7 C.R. 408; *Welk v. Fainbarg* (1967) 255 C.A.2d 269, 276, 63 C.R. 127 [held only an option].)

In *People v. Ocean Shore R. Co.* (1949) 90 C.A.2d 464, 203 P.2d 579, K (first party) made an agreement with M (second party), entitled "option," under which M was given "the exclusive right and option to purchase" certain property on stated installments, with the proviso that on default in an installment K could cancel and retain prior payments, but that K otherwise "shall have no right or claim against second party." *Held*, the agreement was merely an option and not a contract of sale. Despite the fact that M took possession and made regular payments, the language of the instrument showed a studious avoidance of any commitment by M to pay the purchase price, and he could not have been compelled to perform. (90 C.A.2d 469.) (For disapproval of *Ocean Shore* on the issue of whether an option is a compensable interest in condemnation, see 7 *Summary* (10th), *Constitutional Law*, § 1138.)

Source: 1 Witkin, *Summary of California Law* 213 (10th ed., West 2005). Reprinted with permission of West, a Thomson business.

Witkin, *Summary of California Law*, which is usually referred to simply as "Witkin," and *California Jurisprudence, Third Edition* (Cal. Jur. 3d). The two national legal encyclopedias are *Corpus Juris Secundum* (C.J.S.) and *American Jurisprudence, Second Edition* (Am. Jur. 2d). Figure 9-3 contains an excerpt from Witkin. It is a unique source that California attorneys consult more frequently than other encyclopedias, and often more frequently than treatises.[2]

Witkin's *Summary of California Law* is divided into ten volumes, some of which contain only one subject, and others of which contain a number of subjects. The subjects are not organized in alphabetical

---

2. The Witkin Legal Institute publishes other more specialized encylopedias such as *California Criminal Law*, *California Evidence*, and *California Procedure*.

order as in a standard encyclopedia. Rather, the subjects appear in volumes one through ten in the following order: Contracts, Insurance, Workers Compensation, Agency and Employment, Sales, Negotiable Instruments, Secured Transactions in Personal Property, Torts (2 volumes), Constitutional Law (2 volumes), Taxation, Partnership, Corporations, Parent and Child, Husband and Wife, Community Property, Real Property, Personal Property, Equity, Trusts, and Wills and Probate. To find an entry, review the softbound index volume using your research terms. The index will give you a volume number, a subject title, and a section number.

To use a standard legal encyclopedia such as Cal. Jur. 3d or C.J.S., review the softbound index volumes for your research terms. The references will include both an abbreviated word or phrase — the topic — and a section number.[3] The encyclopedia's topic abbreviations are explained in tables in the front of the index volumes. Select the bound volume containing a relevant topic. The spine of each volume includes the range of topics included in that volume.

Next, skim the material at the beginning of that topic for an overview and general information. Then turn to the particular section number given in the index and read the text there. The text of most encyclopedia entries is cursory because the goal of the writers is to summarize the law. National encyclopedia entries will identify significant variations that exist between different jurisdictions, but they do not attempt to resolve differences or recommend improvements in the law. Pocket parts sometimes provide updated commentary.

In addition to describing the law, legal encyclopedias also provide citations to primary authority. California encyclopedias cite California primary authority. In Witkin, important cases and statutes are discussed in the text. In Cal. Jur. 3d, on the other hand, cases and statutes appear in footnotes accompanying the text. Be sure to check the footnotes in encyclopedias for recent, primary authority. Because the footnotes in the national encyclopedias, C.J.S. and Am. Jur. 2d, cite to authorities from all American jurisdictions and tend to be

---

3. Do not confuse these topics and section numbers with the West digest system of topics and key numbers discussed in Chapter 3.

dated, the chance of finding a reference to a recent, relevant case from your jurisdiction in either of them is limited.

An encyclopedia may also contain cross-references to other sources. For example, C.J.S. includes cross-references to relevant topics and key numbers in West's digests. Similarly, Am. Jur. 2d cross-references *American Law Reports*, discussed later in this chapter.

IV. Treatises, Practice Guides, and Other Books

A book on a legal topic can provide an in-depth discussion of the topic and relevant references to primary authority. Legal texts include treatises, practice guides, hornbooks, and *Nutshells*. All of these books share the purpose of covering a particular legal subject, such as contracts or civil procedure. They are distinguished mainly by their level of coverage.

Treatises are generally considered to be more comprehensive statements on a subject than hornbooks, which offer a slightly more summarized view. Practice guides typically cover an area of law thoroughly, but with a particular focus on the nuts and bolts of practice as opposed to the more theoretical approach of treatises or hornbooks. *Nutshells* are a series of books published by West that offer a very condensed explanation of law.

Accordingly, an attorney may use a treatise or practice guide to become familiar with an unfamiliar area of law, while a law student might typically turn to a hornbook or *Nutshell* to prepare for class, or later to gain a better understanding of a class lecture. This chapter focuses on treatises and practice guides because they are more commonly used and cited than hornbooks and *Nutshells*.

A. Treatises

Some treatises are so well known and widely respected that a colleague or supervisor may suggest that you begin research with a particular title. Examples of well-known treatises with a national scope

Table 9-4. Selected Practice Guide Topics

Selected CEB Practice Guides	Selected Rutter Group Practice Guides
California Domestic Partnerships	Alternative Dispute Resolution
California Estate Planning	Bankruptcy
California Juvenile Dependency Practice	Civil Procedure Before Trial
California Land Use Practice	Corporations
California Tort Damages	Federal Civil Procedure Before Trial
Internet Law and Practice in California	Landlord-Tenant
Organizing Corporations in California	Real Property Transactions
Wrongful Employment Termination Practice	

include *Prosser & Keeton on the Law of Torts*, Wright & Miller's *Federal Practice and Procedure*, and *Moore's Federal Practice*.

Treatises are updated in a variety of ways. Bound volumes are updated with pocket parts. Treatises published in looseleaf binders are updated by replacing outdated pages throughout the binder with current material. Each page is dated to show when it was last published. Also, new pages at the beginning of the binders are often printed on different colored paper to draw the reader's attention.

B. California Practice Guides

California lawyers rely heavily on practice guides. Each one covers one area of California law in depth. The authors are typically judges or practitioners with extensive experience in the legal area they are writing about, and the text is practice oriented. Table 9-4 provides a selected list of practice guide topics.

There are four major providers of practice guides in California: Continuing Education of the Bar (CEB), a joint enterprise of the State Bar of California and the University of California, which is the largest publisher of practice guides in California; the Rutter Group, a division of Thomson West, whose guides are often written by judges; Bancroft Whitney, another division of Thomson West; and Matthew Bender, a division of LexisNexis. In addition to traditional practice guides, CEB publishes *Action Guides*, which provide lists of procedures for attorneys to follow in very specific situations such as "Handling Motions to Compel" or "Obtaining a Writ of Attachment." Finally, the California State Bar publishes some practice guides. For a list of the Bar's publications, visit the Bar's website at www.calbar.ca.gov.

National scope practice guides are published by the Practising Law Institute (PLI), the American Law Institute (ALI), and the American Bar Association (ABA).

Practice guides published in looseleaf binders are updated by replacing outdated pages. Some guides are published in hardbound volumes and updated with pocket parts. Still others are republished in full when they need to be updated. Always be sure that you are using the most current material available by checking the library catalog and browsing the shelves nearby.

C. Finding and Using Legal Books

Treatises, practice guides, hornbooks, and *Nutshells* can be located by using a library's catalog and searching for the general subject matter of a research project. For a well-known treatise, include the name of the author as one of the search terms. When searching for practice-oriented material, use the name of publisher (e.g., Continuing Education of the Bar or American Law Institute). After finding one book on point, scan the other titles shelved around it for additional resources.

To use a treatise or other book, begin with either the table of contents or the index. In multi-volume treatises, the index is often in the last volume of the series. Locate your research terms and record the references given. A reference may be to a page number, section number, or paragraph number, depending on the publisher. The table of contents or index should indicate which type of number is referenced. Turn to that part of the book, read the text, and note any pertinent primary authority cited in the footnotes.

The authoritative value of a book depends largely on the reputation of the author. For example, one of the authors of the well-regarded, multi-volume treatise *Marsh's California Corporation Law* is a partner in the high-profile Silicon Valley law firm of Wilson, Sonsini, Goodrich & Rosati. In contrast, a *Nutshell* on corporations is designed as a study guide for students or a quick overview for practitioners; it is not considered authoritative.

V. Legal Periodicals

A. Law Reviews and Law Journals

Law reviews and law journals publish scholarly articles written by law professors, judges, practitioners, and students. Each article covers a specific legal issue in detail. Without the constraints of representing a client's interests or deciding a particular case, an author is able to explore whether the laws currently in force are the best legal rules and to propose changes.

Reading articles published in law reviews and journals can provide a thorough understanding of current law because the authors often explain the existing law before making their recommendations. These articles may also identify weaknesses or new trends in the law that might address your client's situation. The many footnotes in law review and law journal articles can provide excellent summaries of relevant research. Articles written by students are called "Notes" or "Comments." Although not as authoritative as articles written by recognized experts, student articles can provide clear and careful analysis, and their footnotes are valuable research tools.

Some shorter law review pieces, generally written by students, simply summarize a recent case that the publication's editors consider important. These are called "Case Notes" or "Recent Developments." They notify readers of important developments in the law but do not analyze or critique the case in any depth. They are often not helpful beyond offering a short summary of the case and the court's analysis.

Law reviews and law journals are generally published by law students who were selected according to grades or through a competition for membership on the editorial board. Many law reviews have general audiences and cover a broad range of topics; an example is the *McGeorge Law Review*. Many other law journals focus on a specific area of law; examples include the *Hastings Race and Poverty Law Journal* and the *Berkeley Journal of International Law*. Still other law journals are "peer edited," meaning that law professors select and edit the articles to be published. Examples of this type of law journal are the *Journal of Legal Education* and the *Journal of the Association of Legal Writing Directors*.

Periodicals are published first in softbound booklets. Later, several issues will be bound into a single volume. Articles are located by volume number, the name of the journal, and the first page of the article.

Law review and law journal articles are not "updated" in the usual sense. You can, however, find out whether an article has been cited favorably or unfavorably by using a citator such as Shepard's on LexisNexis, KeyCite on Westlaw, or *Shepard's Law Review Citations* in print. Citators are covered in Chapter 8.

B. Bar Journals

Each state's bar journal contains articles of particular interest to attorneys practicing in that state. The California State Bar publishes the *California Bar Journal*. The American Bar Association publishes the *ABA Journal*, which has articles of general interest to attorneys across the nation. Articles in bar journals are often shorter than articles published in law reviews and do not have the extensive footnotes found in law review articles. Moreover, the bar journal articles have a practitioner's focus.

C. Locating Articles

Periodical indexes offer the most accurate way of locating relevant articles. These indexes use specific subject headings into which various articles are classified. Though full-text searching is available on Westlaw, LexisNexis, and other services, full-text searching is likely to produce an unwieldy number of articles, many of which are only tangentially related to your topic.

A popular index of legal periodicals is the *Current Law Index* (CLI). It is available in print and in a database called LegalTrac, which is provided at computer terminals in many law libraries. CLI is also available on LexisNexis and on Westlaw (called "Legal Resource Index"). The coverage of each version varies slightly, but all include articles at least back to 1980.

The other important print index for legal periodicals is the *Index to Legal Periodicals and Books* (ILPB), previously called the *Index to Legal Periodicals*. This index is especially useful in finding older articles because its coverage extends back to the early 1900s. ILPB indexes articles by both subject and author in a single alphabetical list. ILPB volumes are published yearly. They are not cumulative but are updated with softbound pamphlets. Monthly pamphlets are replaced by quarterly pamphlets. These quarterly pamphlets stay on library shelves until an annual bound volume becomes available, sometimes several years later. The ILPB is available online from the HW Wilson Company at www.hwwilson.com, a fee-based site that many libraries provide to their patrons. That site contains indexes for non-legal periodicals, too.

HeinOnline offers full-text searching of a large number of journal articles, although it does not usually contain articles published within the preceding two years. The search engine is not as sophisticated as those available on LexisNexis or Westlaw, but it can be effective. One advantage to retrieving articles from HeinOnline is that the text is provided in PDF format, meaning that pagination looks exactly like the print copy (which makes citation of pinpoint pages easier) and footnotes accompany the relevant text (rather than being placed at the end of the article). Many law school libraries subscribe to HeinOnline, making it free to students and patrons. The website is www.heinonline.org.

VI. *American Law Reports*

American Law Reports (A.L.R.) is a hybrid resource, offering both commentary on certain legal subjects and the full text of a published case on each subject. The commentary articles are called *annotations.* They tend to focus on very narrow topics, take a practitioner's view, and provide a survey of the law in different jurisdictions. Thus, an annotation on the exact topic of your research is likely to be extremely helpful. Annotations are written by lawyers who are knowledgeable, but are not necessarily recognized experts. Each annotation is accompanied by a full-length case.[4] This case may contain different editorial enhancements from those in a reporter, but the court's opinion will be exactly the same. Because cases are so readily available from other sources, most lawyers use A.L.R. almost exclusively for the annotations. The following example demonstrates the link between annotations and cases reported in A.L.R.

> EXAMPLE: An annotation reported at 99 A.L.R.5th 301, written by a lawyer named Dale Joseph Gilsinger, explores one requirement for recovery under the tort "negligent infliction of emotional distress" — the immediacy of the bystander's perception of the accident. The annotation is titled "*Immediacy of Observation of Injury as Affecting Right to Recover Damages for Shock or Mental Anguish from Witnessing Injury to Another.*" The annotation begins with an outline, research references, an index of topics covered, and a table of relevant cases from various jurisdictions, including a lengthy list of California cases. The related case *Groves v. Taylor* is reported on page 693 of the same volume of A.L.R. The parallel citation for that case is 729 N.E.2d 569.

A.L.R. has been published in several series over time. Early series contained both state and federal subjects. Currently, federal subjects are included in A.L.R. Federal, now in its second series. State subjects are discussed in numbered series: A.L.R.3d through A.L.R.6th. To lo-

---

4. While the annotation and case used to be published close together in A.L.R., reported cases now appear in a separate section at the end of each volume.

cate an A.L.R. series in your library, search the library catalog for *American Law Reports.*

Often, the most effective tool for locating annotations using A.L.R. in print is a single-volume Quick Index. One is available for the federal series; another is available for A.L.R.3d through A.L.R.6th. If you are not successful using one of the quick indexes, search the A.L.R Index, a multi-volume reference that covers the more recent numbered series and the federal series together. Another search tool is West's A.L.R. Digest, which includes references to annotations, practice aids, and A.L.R. cases.

A.L.R. annotations are updated with pocket parts. Also check the Annotation History Table in the A.L.R. Index volumes to see whether an annotation has been supplemented or superseded by another annotation, rather than just updated in pocket parts.

VII. Continuing Legal Education Publications

Attorneys in California are required to attend minimum continuing legal education (MCLE) courses every three years to maintain their membership in the State Bar. MCLE rules require active bar members "to remain current regarding the law, the obligations and standards of the legal profession, and the management of their practices."[5]

MCLE courses are led by presenters with significant practice or academic experience, so a presenter may be a practitioner, judge, or law professor. For any course longer than one hour, the presenter must prepare written materials; these could include sample forms, sample documents, and explanations of the law. These written materials must be available either before or during the course itself, and materials provided online must remain available for thirty days following the course.[6] They are not, however, readily available to those who did not take the course.

---

5. St. Bar Cal. R. 2.50.
6. St. Bar Cal. R. 3.501(D).

The various sections of the State Bar offer MCLE courses to their members. In addition, the State Bar of California offers both participatory and self-study MCLE courses through its website and through Versa-Tape Company. The courses are in either audio or video format. A law library may have MCLE courses from other providers on audio or videotape, but these offerings are fairly limited. The written materials provided at MCLEs are not readily available.

Some of the largest national publishers of similar continuing legal education (CLE) materials are the Practising Law Institute (PLI), the American Law Institute (ALI), and the American Bar Association (ABA). Locate CLE material by searching the library catalog by topic or by author, using the names of the more common CLE publishers as search terms.

VIII. Forms

Forms provide shortcuts in legal drafting. When you are drafting a document for the first time in an unfamiliar area of law, a form provides an excellent starting point by keeping you from having to reinvent the wheel.

Forms are available from a diverse range of sources. The website of the California judiciary contains links to a plethora of forms created and approved by the California Judicial Council. The forms cover matters ranging from domestic violence to probate. They are downloadable from the California courts' website at www.courtinfo.ca.gov/forms.

California statutes provide forms for some particular situations. To find statutory forms, search the code index both for the substantive content of the form and under the term "forms." Legal forms may also be found in court rules, in practice guides (covered in Part IV of this chapter), and in CLE materials (discussed in Part VII of this chapter).

A "formbook" may provide actual forms or suggested language that can be used in crafting your document. Examples of California formbooks include *California Forms of Pleading and Practice* (Lexis-Nexis/Matthew Bender) and *California Civil Practice Guide: Civil Procedure Before Trial Forms* (The Rutter Group/Thomson West). Federal forms are available in numerous titles, including *West's Federal Forms* and *American Jurisprudence Legal Forms 2d*. Search the library catalog by subject for topical formbooks.

Take care in using any form. Forms are designed for general audiences, not a particular client. Before using a form, be sure that you understand every word in the form and modify it to suit your client's needs. Do not simply fill in the blanks and assume that the form correctly represents your client's position. Unless a particular form is prescribed by statute or by a court, revise the wording to avoid unnecessary legalese.

IX. Mini-Libraries and Looseleaf Services

A "mini-library" combines both primary and secondary sources under one title. In areas of law like taxation and environmental law, a single title may contain statutes, administrative regulations, annotations to cases and agency opinions, and commentary. The benefit is obvious: all of the material is gathered together so that the researcher does not have to consult multiple sources.

In print, a topical mini-library is often referred to as a looseleaf service because its pages are kept in three-ring notebooks instead of being bound as books. While other secondary sources are also printed in this format, as discussed earlier in this chapter, the term "looseleaf service" refers only to mini-libraries. Again, the looseleaf format allows the publisher to send updates frequently and quickly; the outdated pages are removed and the new pages inserted on a regular basis. A looseleaf service generally fills numerous volumes. The volumes may be arranged by topic, by statute, or by another system.

Looseleaf services always have a "How to Use" section, which generally appears near the beginning of the first volume. Review this section before beginning research. Also consider skimming through a few volumes to become familiar with the organization of that particular service. Pay careful attention to each service's method and frequency of updating.

Beginning research with a looseleaf service is easy when you have a citation to a relevant statute or rule. In tax research, for example, to research a known section of the Internal Revenue Code, simply go to the *Standard Federal Tax Reporter* and find the volume whose spine indicates that the code section is included. In that volume, the statutory language will be followed by regulations issued by the Treasury Department, and then annotations to cases decided by the courts and the Internal Revenue Service. The treatment of that code section will conclude with commentary written by the publisher.

To use a looseleaf when you do not know the particular section that you need to research, begin with the topical index. Often this is the first or last volume of the series. Look up your research terms, and write down the reference numbers given. These references will likely be paragraph numbers rather than page numbers. To maintain indexing despite frequent updates, looseleaf services often are indexed by paragraph number. A "paragraph" may be just a few sentences, several actual paragraphs, or many pages in length. Even though the page numbers will change with future updates, the paragraph reference will remain constant.

Turn to each paragraph number referenced in the index under your key terms. Realize that the paragraph number may be for the statute, regulations, annotations, or commentary. Turn to previous and subsequent pages around that paragraph number to ensure that you have reviewed all relevant material.

Looseleaf services are available online; they are similar to the topical databases available on LexisNexis and Westlaw. Publishers such as Bureau of National Affairs (BNA) and Commerce Clearing House (CCH) gather looseleaf type material together in one database and provide the advantage of full-text searching. For example, the *Standard Federal Tax Reporter* explained earlier is available to subscribers in a database called CCH Tax Research Network. These sites sometimes add more explanations and tools than LexisNexis and Westlaw do, making them more user-friendly to novices.

Online databases often provide tutorials that are helpful introductions to the contents and search techniques unique to each database. Some databases allow you to create a research trail that saves your query words and results. Printing these electronic trails will help you keep track of your research.

X. Restatements

A restatement is an organized and detailed summary of the common law in a specific legal area. While the *Restatement of Contracts* and the *Restatement of Torts* are the titles most familiar to general practitioners, other titles cover a broad range of topics. (See Table 9-5.)

Restatements result from collaborative efforts by committees of scholars, practitioners, and judges organized by the American Law Institute (ALI). These committees, led by a scholar called the *reporter*, draft text that explains the common law in rule format (i.e., they are written with outline headings similar to statutes, rather than in the narrative form of cases). The committees circulate the drafts for review and revision. The restatement that is published by ALI includes not only the text of the rules that embody the common law but also commentary, illustrations, and notes from the reporter.

Restatements were originally intended simply to restate the law as it existed, in an effort to build national consistency in key common

Table 9-5. Restatement Topics

Agency	Property, Mortgages
Conflicts of Law	Property, Servitudes
Contracts	Restitution
Foreign Relations Law	Suretyship and Guaranty
Judgments	Torts, Apportionment of Liability
Law Governing Lawyers	Torts, Products Liability
Property	Trusts
Property, Landlord Tenant	Unfair Competition
Property, Wills and Other	
Donative Transfers	

law areas. Over time, restatements grew more aggressive in stating what the authors thought the law should be.

A portion of a restatement becomes primary authority for a jurisdiction only if it is adopted by a court in a particular case. After a court has adopted a portion of a restatement, the committee's commentary and illustrations, as well as any notes provided by the reporter, may be valuable tools in interpreting the restatement. Cases in other jurisdictions that have adopted the restatement would be persuasive authority.

To find a relevant restatement, search the library catalog for the subject matter or search for "restatement." When working with print volumes, use the table of contents, index, or appendix to find pertinent sections of a restatement. The text of each restatement section is followed by commentary and sometimes illustrations of key points made in the text. Appendix volumes list citations to cases that have referred to the restatement.

A restatement's language is updated only when a later version is published. However, the appendix volumes are updated with pocket parts and supplements, and online restatement databases are kept current. Shepardizing or KeyCiting a restatement section will reveal cases and articles that cite the restatement.

XI. Uniform Laws and Model Codes

Uniform laws and model codes are written by organizations that hope to harmonize the statutory laws of the fifty states. The most active of these organizations is the National Conference of Commissioners on Uniform State Laws (NCCUSL). Much of the work of writing uniform laws and model codes is done by experts who are law professors, judges, legislators, or attorneys.

Familiar examples of these secondary sources include the *Uniform Commercial Code* (UCC) and the *Model Penal Code*. Statutory language is drafted, then comments are solicited, and the language is finalized. The published uniform law or model code includes both the proposed statutory language and explanatory notes from the authors.

Generally, research into a uniform law or model code is relevant only after one of its provisions has been enacted by your jurisdiction's legislature. At that point, the provision becomes primary authority and the explanatory notes become very persuasive secondary authority. That commentary could shed light on a statute in your jurisdiction that was based on the uniform or model language. For example, every state has adopted a version of the UCC. In researching California's commercial code, you could gain insights from commentary on the UCC that discussed the provisions adopted by California. Additionally, the cases of other states that also adopted the same UCC provisions would be highly persuasive in interpreting California's statute.

Uniform laws and model codes, along with official notes and explanations, are published by their authors. Additionally, commercial versions add commentary and often footnotes with case support. West publishes *Uniform Laws Annotated*, which offers indexing, text, and research annotations to uniform laws prepared under the direction of NCCUSL.

Finding a relevant uniform law or model code is similar to finding a restatement. Search the library catalog for the area of law, such as "commercial transactions" or "criminal law"; you may want to include in your search the words "uniform law" or "model code." In the stacks, scan the titles nearby to determine whether more helpful commercial editions have been published. Within the volume or set of volumes containing the uniform law or model code, look in the table of contents, index, and appendix to locate relevant sections. Often they provide section-by-section indexing of the uniform or model provisions, similar to a digest entry.

XII. Jury Instructions

At the close of a trial, the judge instructs the jury. These instructions outline the law; in other words, they tell lawyers what they have to prove in order to prevail. By examining the instructions in advance of trial, an attorney may better be able to present evidence to the jury. Even if a case ends before trial, knowing the instructions a jury would receive may produce more effective research. California civil and criminal jury instructions are available on the California courts website at www.courtinfo.ca.gov; click on "Jury Info." Jury instructions are also available in print form from *California Forms of Jury Instruction* (LexisNexis/Matthew Bender).

XIII. Using Secondary Sources and Practice Aids in Research

As the discussions above suggest, use of the various secondary sources should be tailored to the needs of individual research projects. For a broad overview of an area of law, an encyclopedia may be best. For in-depth analysis of a narrow topic, a law review article is more likely to be helpful. On cutting-edge issues, CLE material often covers new areas of law quickly. In litigation, court-approved forms and uniform jury instructions will be indispensable.

Consider your own background in the subject matter and the goals of your research, and select from these sources accordingly. How many secondary sources you use depends on the success of your early searches and the time available to you. It would almost never be prudent to check every source discussed in this chapter.

Despite the value of secondary sources, they are rarely cited in memoranda or briefs. Some sources, such as indexes for periodicals, are not "authority" at all. Rather, they are authority-finding tools and should never be cited. Encyclopedias, A.L.R. annotations, and MCLE materials should be cited only as a last resort. Even sources that are authoritative, including law review articles and treatises, should be cited only infrequently.

Secondary authorities are typically cited in just three instances. First, sometimes writers need to summarize the development of the law. If no case has provided a summary, citing a treatise or law review article that traces that development could be helpful to the reader. Next, secondary authority may provide additional support for a point already cited to primary authority. For example, you can bolster an argument supported by a case, especially if it is from another jurisdiction, by also citing an article or treatise by a respected expert on the topic. Finally, citation to secondary authority is appropriate when there is no law on point for an argument. When dealing with new areas of the law or when arguing to expand or change the law, your only support may come from a law review article or other secondary authority. Be careful in citing these sources. By citing secondary authorities, you are admitting to your audience that you could not find any primary authority supporting your arguments, which weakens those arguments substantially.

Whether or not you cite a secondary source in a document, you must decide the weight to give secondary authority in developing your own analysis. Consider the following criteria:

- *Who is the author?* The views of a respected scholar, an acknowledged expert, or a judge carry more weight than those of a student author or an anonymous editor.
- *When was the material published?* Especially for cutting-edge issues, a more recent article is likely to be more helpful. Even with more traditional issues, though, be sure that the material analyzes the current state of the law.
- *Where was the material published?* Traditional print sources almost always carry more weight than online websites.
- *Who was the publisher?* Articles published in established law journals are generally granted the most respect. A school's prestige and the length of the journal's existence influence how well established a journal is.
- *What depth is provided?* The more focused and thorough the analysis, the more useful the material will be.
- *How relevant is it to your argument?* If the author is arguing your exact point, the material will be more persuasive than if the author's arguments are only tangential to yours.
- *Has this secondary source been cited previously by courts?* If a court has found an article persuasive in the past, it is likely to find it persuasive again. The text of a secondary source may become primary authority if it is adopted by a court or legislature.

Remember that the goals of reading secondary sources are usually to obtain an overview of an area of law and to locate citations to primary authority. These goals can be met by referring to secondary sources in books in the library or by skimming them online, without the waste of printing out numerous pages of text. Moreover, some lengthy secondary sources — for example, law review articles — may initially seem helpful but after a few pages may concentrate on a narrow point that is not applicable to your situation. When working online, try to avoid printing a document until you are sure that you will need to refer to it repeatedly in your research and analysis.

Chapter 10

Planning a Research Strategy and Organizing Research Results

Every research project needs a defined strategy to ensure thorough and efficient research. This chapter reviews the basic research process, and then discusses how to modify it to design a strategy for particular projects. Then the chapter moves to methods of organizing research results. An organized approach will keep you from getting lost in a sea of papers or online documents and will aid in the analysis of the legal issue.

I. Planning a Research Strategy

The research process presented in Chapter 1 contains seven steps: (1) generate a list of research terms; (2) consult secondary sources and practice aids, including treatises, legal encyclopedias, and law review articles; (3) find controlling constitutional provisions and statutes; (4) find controlling administrative regulations and related administrative law; (5) gather citations to relevant cases and read the cases either online or in print reporters; (6) use citators to update legal authorities; and (7) end research when all analytical points have support and when searches in different sources produce the same set of authorities.

The key to successful research is not to wander randomly through these steps; you might forget a step—and miss an important line of authorities—or you might waste valuable time. Instead, begin each project with a defined strategy that considers the legal clues you have as you begin, the sources available, and the goal of the project. These considerations are addressed below.

A. Asking Fundamental Questions

In developing your strategy, remember to ask the following questions:

- Is this issue controlled by state law, federal law, or both?
- Are there statutes or constitutional provisions on point or is this an area left to common law?
- Are administrative rules or decisions likely to be involved?
- Where in the research process will online sources be more efficient and cost-effective than print sources?
- What period of time needs to be researched?
- How long do I have to complete the project?

Answering these questions and writing out a strategy are likely to make a new project feel less overwhelming because you will see discrete steps that you need to take.

B. Modifying the Strategy

Chapter 1 pointed out a few simple ways that the research process can be modified to suit your research project. To expand on one of those ways, assume that a colleague gives you a citation to a case that is directly on point—a significant clue in your research. You should modify the basic research process to reflect what you know. You might write out a research strategy that looks like the following simple checklist:

- read case
- read statutes and cases it cites
- check digests
- update with KeyCite
- check for additional statutes (generate terms first)
- if statutes are on point, check for administrative law
- if any analytical holes are left, consider secondary sources

Your first step in this project should be reading the case, not generating research terms. Next, you may decide to read some of the key cases cited by that case.

To find even more cases, you could use topics and key numbers from relevant headnotes in the case to search in a West digest (in print or online). Running a KeyCite search would find even more cases and would determine whether the case is still respected authority.

At some point in reading all of these cases, you may have come across a statute. If so, you should stop and read it, and review annotations for more cases that may be relevant. You should also consider whether any administrative regulations have addressed the statute. If you have not yet encountered a statute in your search, you should spend a few minutes searching for one. Now you would need to generate research terms to search in an annotated code.

If you find strong support for all of your analytical points, you might never refer to a secondary source in this project. You may, however, decide to do a quick search of a state-specific treatise or practice guide, just to be sure you have not missed anything.

C. Selecting Sources

As you plan your strategy, decide which sources you will use. You should base this decision primarily on which sources are best suited for the task at hand, though you may also consider availability and personal preference. If, for example, your office has a contract with LexisNexis but not Westlaw, you will naturally choose Shepard's over KeyCite.

1. Researching an Unfamiliar Area of Law

When researching an unfamiliar area of law, you will probably be more successful beginning with secondary sources. Some common research questions and appropriate sources for researching them are discussed next.

a. Typical Practice Issues

Lawyers are faced with fundamental practice tasks every day, such as filing a complaint, conducting depositions, or making a presentation to a client about alternative courses of action. Two very useful tools in these areas are practice guides and state legal encyclopedias. Each is likely to give an overview of the area of law, practice pointers, and even relevant forms and checklists.

b. Cutting-Edge Issues

Often lawyers have to address novel legal issues. (If the answers were easy and clear, a lawyer's knowledge and expertise would be less valued.) Sometimes the new answers can be developed or derived from existing primary authorities, with the addition of some common sense and creativity.

If there is no primary authority on point — consider the first lawyer faced with the question of whether a faxed signature satisfies filing requirements — a secondary source may be the only tool that has addressed the question in a meaningful way. For instance, the author of a recent law review article may have pondered the same question, without having to be concerned about a particular client, and produced thoughtful analysis of the issue.

c. Surveys

Surveys of the law in multiple jurisdictions can be powerful tools in convincing judges to modify existing law in a particular state. Surveys can also help in convincing a court to adopt a new rule favorable to the client when no rule exists in that jurisdiction. A.L.R. annotations usually provide tables that list statutes and cases from every American jurisdiction that has considered a question.

2. Beginning with a Statutory Citation

If you know of a relevant statute, your research project is likely to be most effective if you go directly to an annotated code. In California, you will need to choose between *West's* and *Deering's*, although in practice your choice may be made for you by what is available in your office.

3. Launching from "One Good Case"

If you have one case you know is on point, selecting sources will initially mean deciding whether to work online or in print, which is discussed later. With any case, though, multiple research sources are available. If you are using a print copy published by West, a digest will lead you to additional cases on the same topic by using the topics and key numbers attached to each headnote. On Westlaw, you can use the "Key Numbers" link to browse the digest online or to run a KeySearch through related topics.

On LexisNexis, clicking on a hyperlinked phrase at the beginning of a headnote will lead to a screen for searching by topic for similar cases. Alternatively, clicking on "More Like This Headnote" at the end of the headnote will lead to a screen that allows searching for other cases LexisNexis has indexed under the same topic. Other LexisNexis options include the "More Like This" or "More Like Selected Text" functions located at the top of the screen, which find other cases with similar citations or similar language.

Also, as discussed in Chapter 8, you can use a citator on either Westlaw or LexisNexis to locate cases that have cited the case you already have.

D. Choosing Between Print and Online Research

An important consideration is whether to use print or online sources. Some sources are almost always better in one medium or another, though you must also consider the resources available and your own proficiency in various search techniques.

Sources that are typically preferred in print are secondary sources and statutes. For example, a lawyer specializing in labor law will likely have a deskbook, practice guide, or some other quick reference book close at hand. Referring to that source in print will give the lawyer a head start in understanding the legal issues and thus aid in online research.

Statutory research also lends itself to print sources. Many lawyers find that perusing the print index is more efficient than viewing the index online or constructing full-text searches.

While some lawyers still find print digests preferable to their on-line counterparts, the major providers (LexisNexis and Westlaw) have made such great strides in topic searching that the print versions may not offer much analytical advantage. The key choice here will be based on costs, availability, and your personal preference. In almost all instances, reading cases is more effective in print — either with a reporter or a print-out of cases found online.

E. Sample Research Strategy

To put the discussion above in context, assume that you have been given as a new research task the problem posed in Chapter 1. Your client has suffered nightmares and anxiety attacks after the following scene at a restaurant in San Diego. He and his wife were having lunch at an outside table near the street in the Gaslamp Quarter. The man went inside to use the restroom, and as he was returning to the table he heard a car crash. He saw a table umbrella fall and felt pieces of glass from a falling mirror. A car had jumped the curb and hit his wife. Although she eventually recovered from the serious injuries in-flicted, he has continued to suffer symptoms. He wants to know whether he has a claim against the driver. Assume that you have not researched this issue before and do not know which legal theory he might sue under. A sample strategy is listed in Table 10-1. Of course, you could conduct a very similar search with primarily West prod-ucts, selecting *West's* annotated statutes in Step 3, using KeySearch on Westlaw in Step 5, and updating with KeyCite in Step 6.

Table 10-1. Sample Research Strategy

- Generate terms.
- Check Witkin in print.
- Check for statutes in *Deering's* in print. Review annotations.
- If there are statutes, check for pertinent regulations.
- Skim cases referenced so far. Use LexisNexis Search by Topic for additional cases.
- Shepardize authorities on LexisNexis.
- Create research chart to check analysis.

II. Organizing Research

Legal research often produces many documents that must be organized and analyzed. Keeping research organized is a means to efficient research and thorough legal analysis. Organizational techniques vary among researchers, but the following discussion explains one method that will help novices working on their first projects. This method works for taking notes either on a laptop or on a legal pad. For researchers working with paper and pen, "create a document" simply means turning to a new page in a legal pad.

Before beginning, get a three-ring binder in which you will keep hard copies of the most important authorities you find in your research. Tab the binder with the following headings: strategy/process; list of primary authorities; secondary sources; statutes (include rules and constitutional provisions here); cases; updating; and outline. Consider using color-coded sticky notes to tab each new document so that you can find it easily.

A. Creating a Process Trail and List of Authorities

As you begin research, create a process trail. This document will record what you actually do as you work through the project. Start with your research strategy document and turn it into a quick summary of what you've done. Online providers like LexisNexis and

Westlaw let you print a "Research Trail" or "History" of your work, but it's still a good idea to keep your own process trail that relates to your specific research strategy.

Each time you move to a new step in your research strategy or work with a new resource, make notes in your process trail that summarize your work. For print research, include the volumes you used, the indexes or tables you reviewed, and the terms you searched for. For computer research, include the site, the specific database or link, and the searches that you entered. List both successful and unsuccessful index terms and searches so that (1) you do not inadvertently repeat these same steps later, and (2) you can revisit a seemingly tangential issue that later seems relevant.

Create a list that contains the name and citation for each of the primary authorities that you need to read. Throughout your research, as you come across a potentially relevant authority, include it on the list. This method will allow you to maintain your train of thought with one resource while ensuring that you keep track of important authorities to check later. After creating a list that includes a number of sources, check for duplicates before reading the authorities.

When researching several issues or related claims, consider them one at a time. In this instance, you may have several lists of primary authorities, one for each claim you are researching. You may want to create a different binder for each claim.

B. Taking Analytical Notes

In addition to summarizing the research process, keep notes that summarize your analytical progress. Analytical notes provide a basis for organizing your arguments and writing your document. These notes do not have to be formal or typed; you are likely the only person who will read them.

The notes should be written in your own words, not cut and pasted from the authorities you find. Never underestimate the learning process that occurs while taking notes. Deciding what is important enough to include in notes and expressing those ideas in your own words will increase your understanding of the legal issues involved. Simply printing a document from an online source, highlighting, or cutting and pasting words directly from a source cannot provide this same analytical advantage.

As you find sources that are not relevant, or that duplicate information better provided by another source, make a few notes on your list of authorities. If a source is not relevant, strike through it on the list. On a computer, use the "reviewing" or "commenting" toolbar to strike through irrelevant authorities. Do not completely delete or erase irrelevant authorities or you may later find yourself accidentally reading them again.

Research terms. Too many researchers skip this first step, or they try to do it quickly in their heads. If you know the cause of action—and the various ways that indexes or courts may refer to it—that quick approach may work. But some projects get off to a slow start because the researcher did not begin with a thorough list of research terms. If you do not find pertinent material in your early searches, you may need to go back to the beginning and develop a better list of terms.

Secondary sources. Write a one-page summary for each secondary source you consult. Begin the summary with the title, author, and other citation information for the source. In your own words, summarize the relevant analysis in the source, including references to specific pages. Try to include a few sentences explaining how this source relates to your research.

Enacted law. Because the exact words of constitutions, statutes, and regulations are so important, you should print or photocopy the text of these provisions. Then, to fully understand a complex provision, you should outline it. Highlighting is sufficient only if the text is very short and clear. Be sure to refer to the definition sections of statutes; where important terms are not defined, make a note to look for judicial definitions. Also be sure to read statutes that are cross-referenced in any pertinent statute. Check statutory annotations for cross-references to relevant regulations.

Cases. Brief all relevant cases by explaining their key components in your own words. Be sure you understand the procedural posture and the standard of review applied in each case. Also be sure that you understand the facts of cases. Drawing a time line or a chart of the relationships between the parties may be helpful. Concentrate your effort on the court's reasoning; too many briefs created by novices focus on facts or generate rules, without paying sufficient attention to how the court applied those rules to the specific situation before it. Include the full citation in your brief, and note the pages that points in your brief come from (i.e., include the pinpoint pages that you will have to cite in a written document). Summarize your thoughts on the case: How do you anticipate using this case in your analysis? Which element does it address? Does it resolve certain issues for your problem? Does it raise new questions?

Updating. When you first look at a source online, note its Shepard's or KeyCite symbol. If the symbol is negative, stop to determine whether the source is still good law before basing your analysis on it. Later, carefully update each authority you use in developing your argument. Consider using an "Alert" function in the citator to keep you posted on any changes as you work on your project. If you need to expand your list of authorities, use updating not only to validate sources but also as a research tool. Print lists of citations to compare to the list of authorities in your notebook, which will keep you from duplicating work.

Outlining. Because the most effective research often occurs in conjunction with the analysis of your particular project, try to develop an outline of your client's legal problem as soon as you can. An initial outline may be based on issues listed in a secondary source, the requirements of a statute, or the elements of a common law claim. If outlining feels too restrictive, consider using a flow chart, index cards, or an analysis box. An analysis box is simply a chart that organizes authorities by issue or element; a sample is shown in Table 10-2, following a description of the client's problem earlier in the chapter. The outline or chart should enable you to synthesize the law, apply the law to your client's facts, and reach a conclusion on the desired outcome.

Table 10-2. Sample Analysis Chart

Research Question: Can a client recover against the driver of a car when he heard but did not see the accident that injured his wife?

Issue	Authority	Case Summary	Client Facts	Conclusion
1. Were client and victim "closely related"?	*Thing*	plaintiff must be a relative living in the same house or a parent, sibling, child, or grand-parent of the victim	injured party was client's wife	client was closely re-lated to the victim
2. Was client "present" at the scene and "then aware" of the injury?	*Wilks*	plaintiff must be instantly aware of likely severe injury; was in different room of house when vacuum exploded; met this element	client heard car crash as it happened; was in the adjacent restaurant	client was present be-cause he was close to the crash scene where he had just left his wife and he knew about the crash as it was hap-pening
	Air Crash	plaintiff watched house burn know-knowing family was inside because she'd left minutes before; met this element	client had left his wife at the table moments before	
	Thing	plaintiff was near by when car crash occurred but wasn't aware of it at the time; did not meet this element	client heard crash, saw umbrella fall, and felt mirror pieces	

III. Ending Research

One of the most difficult parts of legal research is knowing when to stop researching. Often deadlines imposed by the court or a supervisor will limit the amount of time spent on a research project. In addition, the expense to the client is always an important consideration.

Apart from these practical constraints, most legal researchers want to believe that if they search long enough they will find a case or statute or article or *something* that answers the client's legal question clearly and definitively. Sometimes that happens; if you find the answer, you know your research is over. Even without finding a clear answer, when your research in various sources leads back to the same authorities, you can be confident that you have been thorough. Review your analytical outline and see whether each point has sufficient support from primary authority in your jurisdiction. As a final checklist, go through each step of the basic research process to ensure you considered each one. Then review your strategy and process trail for this particular project.

If you have worked through the research process and found nothing, it may be that nothing exists. Before reaching that conclusion, expand your research terms and look in a few more secondary sources. Consider whether other jurisdictions may have helpful persuasive authority.

Remember that the goal of legal research is to solve a client's problem. Sometimes the law will not seem to support the solution that your client had in mind. In that situation, think creatively to address the client's problem in a different way. While you must tell your supervisor or your client when a desired approach is not feasible, you will want to have prepared an alternate solution if possible.

Chapter 11

Legal Citation

Lawyers use legal citations to prove that arguments in legal documents are well researched and that analysis is well supported. Legal citations tell the reader where to find the authorities relied on and indicate the level of analytical support the authorities provide.[1] Because citation information is given in abbreviated form, using a uniform and widely recognized format ensures that the reader will understand the information being conveyed.

This chapter addresses the format used to convey citation information. The *California Style Manual*[2] will be explained first. This is the citation manual used by California state courts. Then the chapter will turn to the two national citation manuals, the *ALWD Citation Manual: A Professional System of Citation*[3] and *The Bluebook: A Uniform System of Citation*.[4] A lawyer writing to a state court in Califor-

---

1. In practice documents like office memoranda and court briefs, legal citations are typically included in the text of legal documents rather than being placed in footnotes or listed in a bibliography.

2. Edward W. Jessen, *California Style Manual* (4th ed., West 2000) ("*CSM*") (sometimes referred to as the "gold book" or the "orange book"). In this chapter, footnote references to the *CSM* will be to rule numbers (e.g., *CSM* § 1:2[A]).

3. ALWD & Darby Dickerson, *ALWD Citation Manual* (3d ed., Aspen Publishers 2006) ("*ALWD Manual*"). In this chapter, footnote references to the *ALWD Manual* will include first the rule number and then the page number (e.g., *ALWD* Rule 12.12(a), pages 94–95). Rule numbers are likely to remain the same in subsequent editions, though the page numbers may change.

4. *The Bluebook: A Uniform System of Citation* (The Columbia Law Review et al. eds., 18th ed., The Harvard Law Review Assn. 2005) ("*Bluebook*"). In this chapter, footnote references to the *Bluebook* will include first the rule

nia has the option of using either the *California Style Manual* or the *Bluebook*, but one style of citation must be used throughout the document.[5] The *CSM*, the *ALWD Manual*, and the *Bluebook* are reference manuals, like dictionaries and thesauri. The key to good citation is to learn the general structure of the manual used in your office and to know how to use it, not to read all three manuals cover-to-cover.

I. The *California Style Manual*

A. Orientation to the *CSM*

The first three chapters of the *California Style Manual* cover citations for cases; constitutions, statutes, and rules; and secondary sources. The fourth chapter addresses matters of style (capitalization, quotations, numbers, italics, and punctuation). The final two chapters explain the editorial policies of the official reporters for California cases and case titles.

The *CSM* includes both a table of contents and an index. Both are helpful for finding relevant rules. In addition, each of the six chapters contains a more detailed table of contents. A "Table of Frequently Used Abbreviations" appears at the front of the book, but most of the information is repeated in relevant rules. Those rule-specific lists are often more helpful because similar material can be reviewed quickly. Thus, looking at the list of state and reporter abbreviations in § 1:30 will be easier than looking for each state and reporter in the table in the front of the book.

The rules in the *CSM* result in citations that look a bit different from the citations used in other states or in the national citation manuals. Among the most obvious differences are (1) placement of the entire citation in parentheses, (2) the location of the date immediately after the name of the case, and (3) the use of *supra* in short ci-

---

number and then the page number (e.g., *Bluebook* Rule 18.1.1, pages 151–152). Rule numbers are likely to remain the same in subsequent editions, though the page numbers may change.

5. Cal. R. Ct. Rule 1.200.

Table 11-1. Example Citations from the *California Style Manual*

State Constitution	Cal. Const., art. VI, § 10.
State Statute	Code Civ. Pro. § 340.5.
State Case	*People v. Davis* (1998) 18 Cal.4th 712.
State Rule	Cal. Code Regs., tit. 14, § 916.2.
Law Review Article	Lessig, *The Zones of Cyberspace* (1996) 48 Stan. L.Rev. 1403.

tations. Even with these cosmetic differences, citations under all three citation manuals convey the same essential information. Indeed, the *CSM* relies on the *Bluebook* to fill in any gaps.[6] Examples of California citations are given in Table 11-1. Brief explanations for case and statutory citations follow.

B. Case Citations under the *CSM*

1. Full Citations to Cases

A full citation to a case includes (1) the name of the case, (2) the court that decided the case, (3) the date the case was filed, (4) the volume and abbreviation of the official reporter in which the case was published, (5) the first page of the case, (6) the exact page in the case that contains the idea being cited,[7] and (7) parallel citations.[8]

EXAMPLES: *Brown v. Bd. of Educ.* (1955) 349 U.S. 294, 300 [75 S.Ct. 753, 99 L.Ed. 1083].

People v. Davis (1998) 18 Cal.4th 712, 718 [76 Cal.Rptr.2d 770, 958 P.2d 1083].

---

6. *See e.g. CSM* §§ 1:35, 1:36.

7. This page is commonly called the *pinpoint* or *jump* cite, though the *CSM* uses the term *point* cite. *CSM* § 1:1[E].

8. *CSM* § 1:1.

Use the shortened name of the case from the running head of a print reporter or the shortened name shown in an online source.[9] Words that appear in the table of abbreviations at the front of the *CSM* may be abbreviated; other abbreviations are left to the writer's discretion. See Table 11-5 later in this chapter for a few *CSM* abbreviations, compared to abbreviations used in the national manuals. Between the parties' names, place a lower case "v" followed by a period. Italicize the parties' names and the "v."[10]

Next, in a parenthetical, give the court that decided the case and the jurisdiction, unless both will be clear from the reporter abbreviation.[11] For instance, only decisions of the California Supreme Court are reported in *California Reports,* so citations to that reporter can omit the court and jurisdiction in the parenthetical. Then, in the same parenthetical, give the date the decision was filed.[12]

Following the parenthetical, provide the volume and abbreviation to the relevant print reporter.[13] Abbreviations for California, regional, and federal reporters are included in the table of abbreviations. In addition, abbreviations for California reporters are given in §§ 1:13 through 1:16, abbreviations for regional reporters are listed in § 1:30, and abbreviations for federal cases are given in §§ 1:32[A], 1:33[A], and 1:34[A]. Pay special attention to the series of the reporter, as many reporters are no longer in a first series. Note that no spaces appear between abbreviations of reporter titles (i.e., there's no space between Cal. and 4th). In the *Davis* example above, 18 is the volume number and Cal.4th is the reporter abbreviation for *California Reports, Fourth Series.* The reporters used for California appellate case citations are summarized in Table 11-2.

After the reporter abbreviation, include both the first page of the case and the page containing the idea that you are referencing, sepa-

---

9. *CSM* § 1:1[A].
10. *CSM* § 1:1[B].
11. *CSM* § 1:1[D].
12. *Id.*
13. *CSM* § 1:1[E].

Table 11-2. *CSM* Reporter Abbreviations for
California Appellate Cases

Reporter	California Decisions Reported	Abbreviations
California Reports	Supreme Court	Cal., Cal.2d, Cal.3d, Cal.4th
California Appellate Reports	Court of Appeals	Cal.App., Cal.App.2d, Cal.App.3d, Cal.App.4th
West's California Reporter	Supreme Court Court of Appeals	Cal.Rptr., Cal.Rptr.2d, Cal.Rptr.3d
Pacific Reporter	Supreme Court Court of Appeals through 1960	P., P.2d, P.3d

rated by a comma and a space.[14] The first page of the *Davis* case in the earlier example is 712, and the page containing the specific idea being cited is 718.[15]

In brackets following this required information, you may provide parallel citations.[16] You can also note significant subsequent history.[17]

The citation information above, based on the location of a case in a print reporter, is preferred. If the case is too recent to have been published in a print reporter, or if the case will only be available online, cite it using the name of parties, court, full date, docket number,[18] and the online citation. For example, before the following case

---

14. *Id.*

15. When using an online version of a case, remember that a reference to a specific reporter page may change in the middle of a computer screen or a printed page. Thus, the page number indicated at the top of the screen or printed page may not be the page where the relevant information is located. For example, if the notation *719 appeared in the text before the relevant information, the pinpoint cite would be to page 719, not page 718.

16. *CSM* § 1:1[F]. Including parallel citations is considered better practice. *CSM* § 1:12.

17. *CSM* § 1:11.

18. Docket numbers are explained in *CSM* § 1:17[B].

was available in *Federal Reporter, Third Series*, it could have been cited to Westlaw: *Process Gas Consumers Group v. Federal Energy Regulatory Commission* (D.C. Cir., Oct. 23, 1998, No. 93-1405) ___ F.3d ___ [1998 WL 735869].

2. Short Citations to Cases

After a full citation has been used once to introduce an authority, short citations are subsequently used to cite to the same authority. If a case will be cited frequently, a shortened version of the case name can be used after the full citation. This shortened version may be simply the name of the first party listed.[19]

Within the same paragraph, use *ibid.* to cite the identical page in the case. Use *id.* followed by "at p." and the page number to refer to a different page of the same case. Note that *ibid.* and *id.* can be used only to refer to a case already cited in the same paragraph and only if no other citations have intervened.

> EXAMPLE: In *People v. Davis* (1998) 18 Cal.4th 712, 714, the defendant argued for reversal of a burglary conviction. The defendant had placed a forged check in a chute at a check-cashing business's walk-up facility. *Ibid.* After an extensive review of the crime of burglary in California, the Supreme Court agreed that no burglary had taken place. *Id.* at 724.

To cite a case in a later paragraph (or in the same paragraph after an intervening citation), use the case name, *supra*, the reporter volume and abbreviation, and the relevant page numbers.

> EXAMPLE: *Davis, supra*, 18 Cal.4th at p. 715.

3. Signals

A citation must show the level of support each authority provides. Introductory signals show this support. Note that the strongest

---

19. *CSM* § 1:1[C].

Table 11-3. *CSM* Introductory Signals

No signal	•	The source cited provides direct support for the idea in the sentence.
	•	The citation identifies the source of a quotation.
See	•	The source cited offers indirect support for the idea in the sentence.
	•	The source cited offers support in dicta.
	•	The source cited offers support in a concurring or dissenting opinion.
See also	•	The source cited provides additional support for the idea in the sentence.
	•	The support offered by *see also* is indirect.
E.g.	•	The source cited is representative of other authorities that support the idea explained in the sentence.

support is shown by using no signal. The more common signals are explained in Table 11-3.[20]

4. Explanatory Parentheticals

After a citation, a short parenthetical can help show the relationship between the cited authority and the idea in the text.[21] The most effective parentheticals are very brief descriptions of the facts or holding of the case or short quotes. Complete sentences are disfavored in parentheticals.

EXAMPLE: The California Supreme Court has stated in dicta that inserting a hand into a library chute to steal books would constitute burglary. *See People v. Davis* (1998) 18 Cal.4th 712, 723 (holding that passing a forged check through a chute at a check-cashing business was not burglary).

---

20. *CSM* § 1:4.
21. *CSM* § 1:6.

C. Statutory Citations under the *CSM*

A citation to a California statute requires both the abbreviated name of the code[22] and the section number.[23] Code abbreviations are listed in § 2:8. To show a subdivision of a particular statutory section, use the abbreviation "subd."

A citation to a federal statute includes the title number, code abbreviation, and section number. Subdivisions are shown by enclosing the letter in parentheses. While citation to the official *United States Code* (U.S.C.) is preferred, citation to either *United States Code Annotated* (U.S.C.A.) or *United States Code Service* (U.S.C.S.) is acceptable under the *CSM*. Note that federal statutes do not have code names like California statutes have.

> EXAMPLES: Code Civ. Proc., § 564, subd. (a).
>
> 28 U.S.C. § 1441(a).

D. Quotations

The *CSM* provides clear instruction on quotations: "Quoted material should correspond exactly with its original source in wording, spelling, capitalization, internal punctuation, and citation style."[24] All modifications, additions, or deletions must be shown. The rules for quoted material are provided in *CSM* § 4:12 through § 4:27.

II. National Citation Manuals

The two most widely used national citation manuals are the *ALWD Citation Manual* and the *Bluebook*. Both are large booklets that contain hundreds of pages of citation rules, examples, and explanations.

---

22. *CSM* § 2:8.
23. *CSM* § 2:5[A], 2:6.
24. *CSM* § 4:27.

The *ALWD Manual* is considered by many the best citation manual for novices and for practitioners because it uses a single system of citation for legal memoranda, court documents, law review articles, and all other legal documents. The explanations are clear, and the examples are given in the format required in the memoranda and briefs attorneys write.

The *Bluebook* is the oldest, most widely known citation manual. The difficulty with this manual is that it contains two different citation formats: one for law review footnotes and another for practice documents. Most of the *Bluebook*'s explanations and examples are relevant to law review footnotes, which use different fonts (e.g., italics, large and small capitals) than that used in citations in practice documents. Even so, the *Bluebook* is so well known that most attorneys use the term "Bluebooking" to mean checking citations for consistent format.

A. Navigating the *ALWD Manual* and the *Bluebook*

1. Index

The index at the back of each manual is quite extensive, and in most instances it is more helpful than the table of contents. Most often, you should begin working with a citation manual by referring to the index. In the *Bluebook*, page numbers given in black type refer to citation instructions, while page numbers in blue refer to examples.

2. "Fast Formats" and "Quick Reference"

Many chapters of the *ALWD Citation Manual* begin with citation examples, in tables called "Fast Formats." A list of these "Fast Formats" is provided on the inside front cover of the *ALWD Manual*.

The *Bluebook* contains two "Quick Reference" guides. The one on the inside front cover provides sample citations for law review footnotes. The guide on the inside back cover gives example citations for court documents and legal memoranda. Be sure to consult the appropriate guide for your writing task because the citations differ from one another.

3. Bluebook *"Bluepages"*

The *Bluebook* opens with a section devoted to citations for practitioners. The Bluepages provide information for and additional examples of citations used in documents other than law review articles.[25] When using the *Bluebook*, remember that only the Bluepages and the reference guide at the back of the manual provide examples for practice documents. Thus, a student or lawyer using the *Bluebook* must use the Bluepages to translate other examples from law review format into the format used in practice documents.

4. ALWD *Appendices and* Bluebook *Tables*

The back of each citation manual contains lists of abbreviations and other helpful information. In the *ALWD Manual* these are called "appendices."[26] Pages with dark blue edges at the back of the *Bluebook* contain "tables" with similar information.[27]

B. Citing California Material

Because these manuals are designed for national use, their citations for California material vary from California practice. A summary of abbreviations for California material appears in Appendix 1 (on pages

---

25. The Bluepages are helpful in knowing which font to use in practice document citations. The Bluepages list the following items that should be italicized or underlined in citations in legal memoranda and court documents: case names, titles of books and articles, and introductory signals. Items not included in the list should appear in regular type. Remember to follow the typeface instructions in the Bluepages even when other *Bluebook* examples include large and small capital letters.

26. Especially helpful are Appendix 1 (federal reporters), pages 404–405; Appendix 3 (months, case names), pages 453–461; Appendix 4 (courts), pages 463–470; Appendix 5 (periodicals), pages 471–517; and Appendix 6 (sample memorandum), pages 519–521.

27. Especially helpful are Table T.1 (federal reporters), pages 193–197; Table T.6 (case names), pages 335–337; Table T.12 (months), page 348; and Table T.13 (periodicals), pages 349–372.

Table 11-4. Example California Citations in *ALWD* and *Bluebook* Format

Type of Document	*ALWD* Format	*Bluebook* Format
State Constitution	Cal. Const., art. VI, §10.	Cal. Const., art. VI, §10.
State Statute	Cal. Code Civ. Pro. Ann. §340.5 (West 2006).	Cal. Code Civ. Pro. §340.5 (Deerings 2006).
State Case	*People v. Davis*, 18 Cal. 4th 712, 714 (1998).	*People v. Davis*, 18 Cal. 4th 712, 714 (1998).
State Regulation	Cal. Code Regs., tit. 14, §916.2 (2008).	Cal. Code Regs., tit. 14, §916.2 (2008).
Law Review Article	Lawrence Lessig, *The Zones of Cyberspace*, 48 Stan. L. Rev. 1403 (1996).	Lawrence Lessig, *The Zones of Cyberspace*, 48 Stan. L. Rev. 1403 (1996).

362–364) of the *ALWD Manual* and in Table T.1 (on pages 200–201) of the *Bluebook*. Examples for citations in briefs and memoranda are included in Table 11-4 in this section. Compare these examples to the California citations shown in Table 11-1.

C. Case Citations

1. Full Citations to Cases

In both *ALWD* and *Bluebook* format, a full citation to a case includes (1) the name of the case, (2) the volume and reporter in which the case is published, (3) the first page of the case, (4) the exact page in the case that contains the idea you are citing (i.e., the *pinpoint* or *jump* cite), (5) the court that decided the case, and (6) the date the case was decided.[28] The key points for citation to cases are given below, along with examples.

Include the name of just the first party on each side, even if several are listed in the case caption. If the party is an individual, include

---

28. *ALWD* Rule 12, pages 63–105; *Bluebook* Rule B5.1, pages 6–11.

Table 11-5. Comparison of Selected Abbreviations in *CSM*, *ALWD*, and *Bluebook* Formats

Word	*CSM*	*ALWD* (Appendix 3)	*Bluebook* (Table T.6)
Associate	*	Assoc.	Assoc.
Association	Assn.	Assn.	Ass'n
Center	*	Ctr.	Ctr.
Central	*	C.	Cent.
Community	*	*	Cmty.
Department	Dept.	Dept.	Dep't
Lawyer	Law.	Law.	*
National	Nat.	Natl.	Nat'l
Partnership	*	Partn.	P'ship
Resource[s]	*	*	Res.
University	U. or Univ.	U.	Univ.

* The three manuals do not abbreviate all the same words.

only the party's last name. If the party is a business or organization, shorten the party's name by using abbreviations provided in the citation manual you are using.[29] The *Bluebook*'s abbreviations list is much shorter than the list in the *ALWD Manual*, and some of the abbreviations are slightly different. While the *CSM* abbreviates fewer words than either national manual, its style more often follows that of the *ALWD Manual*. See Table 11-5 in this section for a comparison of abbreviations from the three manuals. Note that in the *Bluebook*, "United States" is never abbreviated when it is a party's name.[30]

---

29. *ALWD* Appendix 3, pages 453–461; *Bluebook* Table T.6, pages 335–337.

30. *Bluebook* Rule 10.2.2, page 86.

Between the parties' names, place a lower case "v" followed by a period. Place a comma after the second party's name, but do not italicize or underline this comma.

The parties' names may be italicized or underlined. Use the style preferred by your office consistently throughout each document.[31] Do not combine italics and underlining in one cite or within a single document.

EXAMPLE: *Flint v. Dennison*, 488 F.3d 816, 820 (9th Cir. 2007).

Next, give the volume and the reporter in which the case is found.[32] Always note carefully whether the reporter is in its first, second, third, or fourth series.[33] In the *Flint* example above, 488 is the volume number and F.3d is the reporter abbreviation for *Federal Reporter, Third Series.*

After the reporter name, include both the first page of the case and the pinpoint page containing the idea that you are referencing, separated by a comma and a space.[34] The first page of the *Flint* case above is 816, and the page containing the specific idea being cited is 820. If the pinpoint page you are citing is also the first page of the case, then the same page number will appear twice.[35]

---

31. *ALWD* Rule 12.2 (case names), page 64 and Rule 1.1 (typeface choice), page 13; *Bluebook* Rule B2, page 4.

32. For cases available only on LexisNexis or Westlaw, follow *ALWD* Rule 12.12(a), pages 94–95 and *Bluebook* Rule B5.1.3, page 10 and Rule 18.1.1, pages 151–152.

33. Abbreviations for common reporters are found on page 77 of the *ALWD Manual*; abbreviations for reporters for California cases are included on pages 362–364. The *Bluebook* does not have a comprehensive list of common reporters; check Table T.1 on pages 193–242 for reporters in a particular jurisdiction. Abbreviations for reporters for California cases are given in the *Bluebook* on pages 200–201.

34. *ALWD* Rule 5, pages 33–36 and Rule 12.5, pages 82–83; *Bluebook* Rule B5.1.2, page 7.

35. When using an online version of a case, remember that a reference to a specific reporter page may change in the middle of a computer screen or a printed page. *See* note 15 *supra.*

In a parenthetical following this information, indicate the court that decided the case.[36] In Appendix 1 of the *ALWD Manual* and in Table T.1 of the *Bluebook*, the notations for the courts of each jurisdiction are included in parentheses just after the name of the court. In the *Flint* example, the Ninth Circuit Court of Appeals, a federal court, decided the case.

If the reporter abbreviation clearly indicates which court decided a case, do not repeat this information in the parenthetical. To give an example, only cases of the United States Supreme Court are reported in *United States Reports*, abbreviated U.S. Repeating the court notation (U.S.) in citations to that reporter would be duplicative. By contrast, *Pacific Reporter, Third Series*, abbreviated P.3d, publishes decisions from different courts within several states, so the court that decided a particular case needs to be indicated parenthetically. Thus, in the second example below, "Cal." indicates that the decision came from the California Supreme Court rather than from another court whose decisions are also published in this reporter.

EXAMPLES: *Brown v. Bd. of Educ.*, 349 U.S. 294, 300 (1955).

Ketchum v. Moses, 17 P.3d 735, 736 (Cal. 2001).

Because *West's California Reporter* publishes cases from both the California Supreme Court and the California Courts of Appeal, all citations to that reporter have to include the court designation in the parenthetical.

When citing to Court of Appeal cases published in *West's California Reporter*, the *ALWD Manual* requires that the district be included,[37] whereas the *Bluebook* says not to include that information.[38]

ALWD EXAMPLE: *People v. Wise*, 30 Cal. Rptr. 2d 413
                        (App. 1st Dist. 1994).

BLUEBOOK EXAMPLE: *People v. Wise*, 30 Cal. Rptr. 2d 413
                        (Ct. App. 1994).

---

36. *ALWD* Rule 12.6(a), page 83; *Bluebook* Rule B5.1.3, page 8.
37. *ALWD* Rule 12.6(b)(2).
38. *Bluebook* Rule 10.4(b).

The final piece of required information in most cites is the date the case was decided. For cases published in reporters, give only the year of decision,[39] not the month or date.[40]

Prior and subsequent history can be added to the end of a citation, as shown in the example below.[41]

> EXAMPLE: The only time that the Supreme Court addressed the requirement of motive for an EMTALA claim, the court rejected that requirement. *Roberts v. Galen of Va.*, 525 U.S. 249, 253 (1999), *rev'g* 111 F.3d 405 (6th Cir. 1997).

2. Short Citations to Cases

After a full citation has been used once to introduce an authority, short citations are subsequently used to cite to the same authority.[42] When the immediately preceding cite is to the same source and the same page, use *id.* as the short cite. When the second cite is to a different page within the same source, follow the *id.* with "at" and the new pinpoint page number. Capitalize *id.* when it begins a citation sentence, just as the beginning of any sentence is capitalized.[43]

If the cite is from a previously cited case that is not the immediately preceding cite, give the name of one of the parties (generally the first party named in the full cite), the volume, the reporter, and the pinpoint page following "at."[44] The format "*Davis* at 714" consisting

---

39. *ALWD* Rule 12.7, pages 86–87; *Bluebook* Rule B5.1.3, page 8 and Rule 10.5, pages 90–91.

40. For cases available only online, give the month abbreviation, date, and year. *ALWD* Rule 12.12(a), pages 94–95; *Bluebook* Rule B5.1.3, page 10 and Rule 18.1.1, pages 151–152.

41. *ALWD* Rules 12.8–12.10, pages 87–92; *Bluebook* Rule B5.1.5, pages 10–11.

42. *ALWD* Rules 11.2 and 11.3, pages 52–56; *Bluebook* Rule B5.2, pages 11–13.

43. *ALWD* Rule 11.3(d), page 55; *Bluebook* Rule B5.2, page 12.

44. *ALWD* Rule 11.2, pages 52–53 and Rule 12.21(b), pages 102–103; *Bluebook* Rule B5.2, page 11.

of just a case name and page number, is incorrect. The volume and reporter abbreviation are also needed.

> EXAMPLE: In *People v. Davis*, 18 Cal. 4th 712, 714 (1998), the
> defendant argued for reversal of a burglary conviction. The de-
> fendant had placed a forged check in a chute at a check-cashing
> business's walk-up facility. *Id.* After an extensive review of the
> crime of burglary in California, the Supreme Court disapproved
> *People v. Ravenscroft*, 198 Cal. App. 3d 639 (2d Dist. 1988), on
> which the prosecution had relied, and agreed that no burglary
> had taken place. *Davis*, 18 Cal. 4th at 724.

D. Federal Statutory Citations

The general rule for citing federal laws is to cite the *United States Code* (U.S.C.), the official code for federal statutes.[45] Because that series is published so slowly, the current language will most likely be found in a commercial version, either *United States Code Annotated* (U.S.C.A., published by West) or *United States Code Service* (U.S.C.S., published by Lexis Publishing).

A cite to a federal statute includes the title number, code abbreviation, section number, publisher (except for U.S.C.), and date. The date given in statutory cites is the date of the volume in which the statute is published, not the date the statute was enacted. If the language appears only in the pocket part, include only the date of the pocket part.[46] If the language of only a portion of the statute is reprinted in the pocket part, include the dates of both the bound volume and the pocket part.[47]

---

45. *ALWD* Rule 14, pages 111–115; *Bluebook* Rule B6.1.1, pages 13–15.
46. *ALWD* Rule 8.1, page 45; *Bluebook* Rule 3.1, page 58.
47. *ALWD* Rule 14.2, pages 111–115; *Bluebook* Rule 12.2.2, page 103.

EXAMPLE: 14 U.S.C.A. § 736 (West Supp. 2007).

(Statutory language appears in the supplemental pocket part only)

EXAMPLE: 14 U.S.C.A. § 740 (West 1990 & Supp. 2007).

(Statutory language appears in both the bound volume and the supplemental pocket part)

E. Signals

As noted in the discussion of California citation, introductory signals show the type of support each authority provides. The more common signals are explained in Table 11-2.[48]

F. Explanatory Parentheticals

Similar to parentheticals under the *CSM*, both the *ALWD Manual* and the *Bluebook* provide for explanatory parentheticals following citations.[49] Sometimes this parenthetical information conveys to the reader the weight of the authority (e.g., a case may have been decided *en banc* or *per curiam*). Or the case may have been decided by a narrow split among the judges who heard the case.[50] Parenthetical infor-

---

48. *ALWD* Rule 44, pages 323–327; *Bluebook* Rule B4, pages 4–5.

49. *ALWD* Rule 46, pages 335–337; *Bluebook* Rule B5.1.4, page 10 and Rule B11, pages 22–23. The rules for explanatory parentheticals are similar in the two citation manuals. However, the *Bluebook* rule states that parenthetical information generally should not be given in a complete sentence, but should begin with a present participle (i.e., a verb ending in "-ing") that is not capitalized. *Bluebook* Rule B11, page 22. The *ALWD Manual* is more flexible about the format of parentheticals. *See ALWD* Rule 46.3, page 337.

50. *ALWD* Rule 12.11(b), page 94; *Bluebook* Rule B5.1.4, page 10.

mation also allows you to name the judges who joined in a dissenting, concurring, or plurality opinion.[51]

> EXAMPLE: Excluding relevant evidence during a sentencing hearing may deny the criminal defendant due process. *Green v. Georgia*, 442 U.S. 95, 97 (1979) (per curiam) (regarding testimony of co-defendant's confession in rape and murder case).

When using this type of parenthetical, be sure that you do not inadvertently hide a critical part of the court's analysis at the end of a long citation, where a reader is likely to skip over it.

G. Quotations

In every citation system, the words, punctuation, and capitalization of a quote must appear exactly as they are in the original.[52] Any alterations or omissions must be indicated. Include commas and periods inside quotation marks; place other punctuation outside the quotation marks unless it is included in the original text. Also, try to provide smooth transitions between your text and the quoted text.

H. Additional Citation Details

The following citation details are second nature to users of the national manuals, though they frequently trip up both students and practitioners familiar with a particular state's citation rules.

- *Numbers.* It is most common in legal documents to spell out numbers zero through ninety-nine and to use numerals for

---

51. *ALWD* Rule 12.11(a), page 93; *Bluebook* Rule B5.1.4, page 10.

52. *ALWD* Rules 47, 48, and 49, pages 341–355; *Bluebook*, Rule 5, pages 68–71. There is one slight difference in the quotation rules: For the *Bluebook*, quotations that have fifty or more words must be set off in indented blocks. *Bluebook* Rule 5.1, page 68. That means the writer must count words to know how many words the quotation contains. In contrast, the *ALWD Manual* requires indented blocks for quotes that are fifty or more words *or* quotes that span four or more lines of typed text. *ALWD* Rule 47.5(a), page 344.

larger numbers. However, always spell out a number that is the first word of a sentence.[53]

- *Ordinal abbreviations.* The most confusing are 2d for "Second" and 3d for "Third" because they differ from the common non-legal formats 2nd and 3rd.[54]
- *Spacing of abbreviations.* Do not insert a space between abbreviations of single capital letters. For example, there is no space in U.S. Ordinal numbers like 1st, 2d, and 3d are considered single capital letters for purposes of this rule. Thus, there is no space in P.2d or F.3d because 2d and 3d are considered single capital letters. Leave one space between elements of an abbreviation that are not single capital letters. For example, F. Supp. 2d has a space on each side of "Supp."[55]

III. *Bluebook* Citations for Law Review Articles

While the rules discussed above also apply to citations in footnotes to law review articles following the *Bluebook*, that manual uses different fonts—including large and small capital letters—for law review footnote citations. The example in Table 11-6 shows a statutory citation using the *ALWD Manual*, the *Bluebook* format for legal memoranda and court documents, and the *Bluebook* format for law review footnotes.

Table 11-6. Comparison of *ALWD* and *Bluebook* Formats

ALWD Manual	Bluebook	
All Documents	Legal Memoranda	Law Review Articles
Cal. Penal Code Ann. §451 (West 1999).	Cal. Penal Code §451 (West 1999).	Cal. Penal Code §451 (West 1999).

---

53. *ALWD* Rule 4.2, pages 29–32; *Bluebook* Rule 6.2(a), page 73.
54. *ALWD* Rule 4.3, page 32; *Bluebook* Rule 6.2(b), page 74.
55. *ALWD* Rule 2.2, pages 16–17; *Bluebook* Rule 6.1, page 72.

Using the *Bluebook* to write citations for law review articles is considerably easier than using it for practice documents because almost all of the examples given in the *Bluebook* are in law review format. Table 11-7 of this chapter summarizes the typeface used for several common sources and gives examples.

Law review articles place citations in footnotes or endnotes, instead of placing citations in the main text of the document.[56] Most law review footnotes include text in ordinary type, in italics, and in large and small capital letters.[57] This convention is not universal, and each law review selects the typefaces it will use. Some law reviews may use only ordinary type and italics. Others may use just ordinary type.[58] Assuming you are submitting an article to a law review that uses all three typefaces, *Bluebook* Rule 2 dictates which typeface to use for each type of authority.

The typeface used for a case name depends on (1) whether the case appears in the main text of the article or in a footnote and (2) how the case is used. When a case name appears in the main text of the article or in a textual sentence of a footnote, it is italicized. By contrast, if a footnote contains an embedded citation, the case name is written in ordinary type. Similarly, when a full cite is given in a footnote, the case name is written in ordinary type. But when a short cite is used in footnotes, the case name is italicized.

IV. Citations Not Covered by a Manual

As comprehensive as the *CSM*, the *ALWD Manual*, and the *Bluebook* are, they do not definitively answer every citation question. When you cannot find a specific rule to cover a source you need to cite, look for rules regarding analogous sources. In creating a citation, always be guided by the purpose of citation: to allow a reader to find a source and to understand the type and weight of support it provides.

---

56. *Bluebook* Rule 1.1(a), page 45.
57. *Bluebook* Rule 2.2(a), page 56.
58. *Bluebook* Rule 2.1, pages 54–56.

Table 11-7. *Bluebook* Typeface for Law Review Footnotes

Item	Type used	Example
Cases	Use ordinary type for case names in full citations. (See text for further explanation.)	Legal Servs. Corp. v. Velazquez, 531 U.S. 533 (2001).
Books	Use large and small capital letters for the author and the title.	DAVID S. ROMANTZ & KATHLEEN ELLIOTT VINSON, LEGAL ANALYSIS: THE FUNDAMENTAL SKILL (1998).
Periodical articles	Use ordinary type for the author's name, italics for the title, and large and small capitals for the periodical.	Linda Berger, *Lies Between Mommy and Daddy: The Case for Recognizing Spousal Emotional Distress Claims Based on Domestic Deceit that Interferes with Parent-Child Relationships*, 33 LOY. L.A. L. REV. 417 (2000).
Explanatory phrases	Use italics for all explanatory phrases, such as *aff'g, cert. denied, rev'd*, and *overruled by*.	Legal Servs. Corp. v. Velazquez, 531 U.S. 533 (2001), *aff'g* 164 F.3d 757 (2d Cir. 1999).
Introductory signals	Use italics for all introductory signals, such as *see* and *e.g.* when they appear in citations, as opposed to text.	*See id.*

Selected Bibliography

California Research

Larry D. Dershem, *California Legal Research Handbook* (2d ed., W.S. Hein & Co. 2008).

John K. Hanft, *Legal Research in California* (6th ed., West 2007).

Daniel W. Martin, *Henke's California Law Guide* (5th ed., Lexis 1999).

California Citation

Susan Heinrich, *Using the California Style Manual and The Bluebook: A Practitioner's Guide* (West 2000).

Edward W. Jessen, *California Style Manual* (4th ed., West 2000).

General Research (tending to focus on federal material)

Robert C. Berring & Elizabeth A. Edinger, *Finding the Law* (12th ed., West 2005).

Morris L. Cohen & Kent C. Olson, *Legal Research in a Nutshell* (8th ed., West 2003).

Christina L. Kunz et al., *The Process of Legal Research* (6th ed., Aspen Publishers 2004).

Roy M. Mersky & Donald J. Dunn, *Fundamentals of Legal Research* (8th ed., Found. Press 2002).

Laurel Currie Oates & Anne Enquist, *Just Research* (Aspen Publishers 2005).

Amy E. Sloan, *Basic Legal Research: Tools and Strategies* (3d ed., Aspen Publishers 2006).

Legal Analysis

Charles R. Calleros, *Legal Method and Writing* (5th ed., Aspen Publishers 2006).

Linda H. Edwards, *Legal Writing: Process, Analysis, and Organization* (4th ed., Aspen Publishers 2006).

Linda H. Edwards, *Legal Writing and Analysis* (2d ed., Aspen Publishers 2007).

Richard K. Neumann, Jr., *Legal Reasoning and Legal Writing: Structure, Strategy, and Style* (5th ed., Aspen Publishers 2005).

Laurel Currie Oates, Anne Enquist & Kelly Kunsch, *The Legal Writing Handbook: Analysis, Research, and Writing* (4th ed., Aspen Publishers 2006).

Mary Barnard Ray & Barbara J. Cox, *Beyond the Basics: A Text for Advanced Legal Writing* (2d ed., West 2003).

David S. Romantz & Kathleen Elliott Vinson, *Legal Analysis: The Fundamental Skill* (Carolina Academic Press 1998).

Helene S. Shapo, Marilyn R. Walter & Elizabeth Fajans, *Writing and Analysis in the Law* (5th ed., Found. Press 2008).

About the Authors

Hether C. Macfarlane directs the Legal Process Program at Pacific McGeorge School of Law. She is a graduate of Albany Law School, and she directed the Legal Research and Writing Program there for three years. She practiced law at the Washington, DC office of Hunton & Williams, specializing in environmental and administrative law.

Suzanne E. Rowe began her legal career clerking for The Honorable Rudi M. Brewster of the Southern District of California. She has taught legal research and writing at the University of San Diego School of Law, Florida State University College of Law, and the University of Oregon School of Law. She is a graduate of Columbia University School of Law.

Index